Culture has shriveled hope into nothing more than a wishful, weary want, as something that lives in a near-impossible future. Yet, hope in Christ is living, breathing, pulsing, and inhabiting the space we navigate (no matter how routine). Ashley's vulnerability invites readers to see God's great glory in the bits and psieces of the ordinary, encouraging us to not merely trudge through our days but to know that they matter in this life and the next. In a world that whispers hope is only for the lucky ones, Ashley reminds us that hope is available for us all, right here and right now.

—Peyton Garland, author of
Tired, Hungry, & Kinda Faithful and Not so by Myself

This book is no small thing. I have watched Ashley live out every word in this book as she grew in confidence and in the knowledge of God and later as she began boldly sharing this with our church family. It is a joy to see her expand her gift to write this beautiful book. This is not a self-help book, this is your best friend sitting down over a cup of tea and graciously opening her Bible. Sharing God in practical, relatable, and life-changing ways. If you've ever wondered what your small contribution was worth, this book will open your eyes to how big small can be.

—Mary Turner, Co-Lead Pastor of City Church

No matter who you are, at one point or another, we all find ourselves questioning our significance. Does what I do matter? In *No Small Thing*, Ashley weaves a rich tapestry of biblical truth that resoundingly answers that question. She invites us to see not only God's faithfulness but God's closeness to us — liberating each of us to open our eyes to the gift that our everyday and ordinary lives are.

—Tabitha Panariso, writer and therapist

Ashley has written a book I truly needed right now, in this very season of life! *No Small Thing* reminds us that being fully present and faithful to God in the ordinary moments of our day really is a big deal and does, in fact, matter for eternity. If you've ever wondered if your life is "too small a thing," you'll be encouraged by the personal stories and truths from Scripture that Ashley shares as she explains the power of living with our gaze set on Him.

—Amy Hale, writer and speaker

With vulnerability, wisdom, and a firm grasp on Scripture, Ashley Kelly tackles the questions we all inevitably find ourselves asking at some point: Do I matter? Does my work matter? Are any of the things that fill my days even important? The answer you'll discover as you read is a resounding "yes"—not so much because of who we are, but because of who God is. Whether you're a stay-at-home mom, a CEO, or something in-between, in Ashley you'll find a worthy guide who has wrestled with what it means to show up for today and value what God has entrusted us with. Anchoring us in a much bigger story than our own, *No Small Thing* will take you on a practical journey of discovery and propel you towards a life of satisfying purpose, helping you find significance and joy right where you are.

—Aimée Walker,
Founder of The Devoted Collective and author of *But I Flourish*

No Small Thing

No Small Thing

finding freedom and significance
in the right here, right now of life

Ashley Kelly

No Small Thing

Copyright© 2023 by Ashley Kelly
Library of Congress Cataloging-in-Publication Data
Library of Congress Number: 2023911447 | ISBN: 978-1-961732-00-1 (ebook) | ISBN: 979-8-9878343-9-8 (paperback) | ISBN: 978-1-961732-01-8 (print)

Scripture quotations marked (ESV) are taken from the ESV® Bible (The Holy Bible, English Standard Version®), copyright © 2001 by Crossway, a publishing ministry of Good News Publishers. Used by permission. All rights reserved. The ESV text may not be quoted in any publication made available to the public by a Creative Commons license. The ESV may not be translated in whole or in part into any other language.

Scripture quotations marked (NIV) are taken from the Holy Bible, New International Version®, NIV®. Copyright © 1973, 1978, 1984, 2011 by Biblica, Inc.™ Used by permission of Zondervan. All rights reserved worldwide. The "NIV" and "New International Version" are trademarks registered in the United States Patent and Trademark Office by Biblica, Inc.™

Scripture quotations marked (NLT) are taken from the Holy Bible, New Living Translation, copyright ©1996, 2004, 2015 by Tyndale House Foundation. Used by permission of Tyndale House Publishers, Carol Stream, Illinois 60188. All rights reserved. Scripture quotations marked (MSG) are taken from The Message, copyright © 1993, 2002, 2018 by Eugene H. Peterson. Used by permission of NavPress. All rights reserved. Represented by Tyndale House Publishers.

Any internet addresses (website, blogs, etc.) and telephone numbers in this book are offered as a resource. They are not intended in any way to be or imply an endorsement from Called Creatives Publishing, not does Called Creatives Publishing vouch for the content of these sites and numbers for the life of this book.

All rights reserved. No portion of this book may be reproduced or shared in any form – electronic, printed, photocopied, recording, or by any information storage or retrieval system, without prior written permission from the author. The use of short quotations is permitted.

Published in association with Called Creatives Publishing, www.calledcreativespublishing.com

Cover design: Called Creatives Publishing
Interior design: Ashley Kelly

2023 – First Edition

To my mom.

Mom, it all matters.
Every little thing.
I would not be who I am or
where I am today if it weren't for *you*.

Thank you.
I love you.

*When I look at your heavens, the work of your fingers,
the moon and the stars, which you have set in place,
what is man that you are mindful of him,
and the son of man that you care for him?*

PSALM 8:3-4 ESV

―――――――――――

*God, teach me lessons for living
so I can stay the course.
Give me insight so I can do what you tell me—
my whole life one long, obedient response.*

PSALM 119:33-34 MSG

CONTENTS

Start Here: Small Doesn't Mean Insignificant 1
Chapter 1: Is It Too Small a Thing? 7

—Tamar's Story— 15

PART 1: Is It Too Small a Thing ...Who God is and What He has Done? 19
Chapter 2: Big God 21
Chapter 3: Big Plan 35
Chapter 4: Big Hope 51

—Rahab's Story— 67

PART 2: Is It Too Small a Thing ...What is in Front of You? 71
Chapter 5: Finding Beauty in the Ordinary 73
Chapter 6: Everyday Faithfulness Matters 89
Chapter 7: The Ministry of Small Things 109

—Ruth's Story— 129

PART 3: Is It Too Small a Thing ...What God is Asking of You? 133
Chapter 8: A Little Leading Goes a Long Way 135
Chapter 9: One Obedient Step at a Time 155
Chapter 10: It's Out of Your Control 175

—Bathsheba's Story— 195

Conclusion: It Is No Small Thing 198

Dear Reader 203
Acknowledgments 205

Start Here

Small Doesn't Mean Insignificant

Does any of this really matter?

How could my ordinary, often messy and mundane, everyday life have any significance?

Today looks so much like yesterday, and tomorrow is shaping up to be the same. Maybe someday in the future—you know, eventually, when I get "there"—my days will matter. Perhaps someday, my days will hold meaning, be fulfilling, or be what I always thought they would be.

For now, though, I'm just not sure my day-to-day, my menial and monotonous mornings, my humdrum afternoons, and my predictable evenings amount to much. I'm not sure the right here, right now of my life means much at all—other than keeping my children and husband alive.

Does any of this really matter?

Do I even matter?

I sure hope I am not the only one who has been plagued with thoughts similar to these. The nagging questions may not always be so melodramatic, but I'll be honest; there have been days I could seriously lean into it!

Before you put this book down, assuming it's not for you, I hope you'll reconsider. The struggle for significance does not discriminate; it can show up in any season of life. Whether you are a wide-eyed young adult ready to make your mark on the world or a stay-at-home mom tucked away in the rhythm of everyday motherhood, the siren song of significance plays for you.

Maybe you're a single thirty-something surrounded by married moms and struggling to embrace where you are not. Perhaps you are an empty nester, trying to find your place in the world without your chickadees by your side. Maybe you are what my church calls a "classic"—someone well-seasoned in life—yet you're not ready to throw in the towel! You still have much fight (the good kind) left in you, but what can you do now?

My friend—that's what I will call you from here on out—you are so much more than what you do and don't do, what you have and don't have, or what you do or don't allow to determine your value. Your significance is never in question! Your worth was set in stone the moment Jesus Christ—God almighty, who stepped into creation, covered in flesh with blood pumping through His veins—sacrificed His life and poured out His blood for you.

If your significance is settled and sure, then you'd better believe that every day matters, however small or commonplace it may seem. Significance isn't meant to be found someday; significance is for today, is *in* your today. Right here, right now is what you have! Right here, right now is where you are!

Right here. Right now.

An Origin Story

Everybody loves an origin story, right? Well, this is not the beginning of *my* story, but it is the genesis of the battle cry living in my heart for you, me, and all of us.

Gripping a microphone in one hand and my husband's hand in the other, my heart skipped a few beats as the music faded and all eyes turned to us. It was an early June evening in 2019, and we were standing on the stage of our church in my hometown in good ol' Oklahoma. Being a pastor, my husband was used to this—microphone in hand, sharing his heart or other pertinent information. Me? It had been a couple of years since my time as the children's ministry director and consistent public speaking. Despite the nerves, I could sense the weight of this moment, fully convinced that what I was about to share was true.

I just had no idea how much my words would impact *me* or the personal journey I would soon find myself experiencing.

"Small doesn't mean insignificant."

I declared that after my husband announced our church's intention to start a new campus. Our lead pastors, along with my husband, had sensed a nudge toward starting a campus in a small town twenty-five miles from our current campus. Yes, a small town—a tiny, rural town with roughly 3,500 people. In a time when it is customary and even expected of churches to focus on big cities and move toward centralized hubs of people, we were going small.

NO SMALL THING

We live in a culture that equates size with significance. We think big equals important, often viewing small as inferior, broken, or worthless. But here's the truth about small things that I boldly proclaimed that summer evening: I believe God can use something small, even a small town in Oklahoma, to change the world.

In fact, He did it before in a huge way.

Jesus spent most of his childhood in Nazareth and became known as Jesus *of* Nazareth—a tiny, unremarkable town set in the shadows of larger, seemingly more important cities. One of Jesus's soon-to-be disciples even asked, "Can anything good come out of Nazareth?" (John 1:46 ESV). Yet, God saw fit to send His Son—our Savior, Lord, and King—to live in this small, overshadowed, and overlooked town. Jesus's life and what He did for the world were not insignificant. (I hope we can all agree on that!)

Who is to say that any small town is too small for God to move through and do what He will in the lives of the people He loves? We serve a God who can do immeasurably more than we could ever ask, imagine, or dream (Ephesians 3:20). In His limitlessness, God does not view size and stature the same as we, limited humans, do.

Friend, you may not live in a small town, but maybe you feel small in another way. You may question your worth and value in the overwhelming world we live in today. You may feel hidden and unseen as you struggle to show up for your family, work, or friends. Maybe you wonder how your regular, everyday life holds any significance in light of all the daunting national and world news. This same truth applies to you, too. Small doesn't mean insignificant. *You* are not insignificant. (God has already settled that!)

SMALL DOESN'T MEAN INSIGNIFICANT

What is in front of you—the people, the places, and your life right now—is no small thing.

What God may be asking of you—whether simple and ordinary or bold and new—is no small thing.

Though vast and mighty, God sees, knows, and loves you. While it's true that He holds the universe in His hands, He also cares deeply about the intricate details of your life. And guess what? He's calling you to do the same.

Small doesn't mean insignificant.

These words continue to encourage me today, and I sincerely hope they do the same for you. It is a truth God opened my eyes to in life, His Word, and the way of His Kingdom. In recognizing these few words as God-proven truth, I have found freedom to pursue not *my* plan but *His* plan for my life, freedom to follow and obey even in—especially in—the small things.

In short, I have found freedom and significance in the right here, right now of life.

And I believe you can, too.

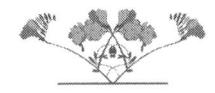

Chapter 1
Is It Too Small a Thing?

As she hobbled her way down the aisle, clutching two meager coins in her pocket, did she wonder, "Will this be enough? What little I have to offer, will it be acceptable?"

Clink. Clinkety-clunk. Clink clink clink. Clunk.

The sounds of the offerings poured in from the wealthy men and women ahead of her nearly drowned out her resolve to move forward. Nearly. But something kept her going. Something urged her onward.

As she neared the offering box, she saw him from the corner of her eye: The one everyone had been talking about, whose name was whispered by some like a blessing and others like a curse. He was sitting right there, and his eyes were on her.

The woman stepped up, head down and hands firmly gripping those two meager coins. As she placed her little offering in the box, no sound reverberated. No clinking. And no clunking.

Silence.

Everyone must have known what little she had to give. There was no hiding it.

Did the poor widow walk away with tears in her eyes? Did she brave a look toward the man surrounded by his disciples? Did she hear him proclaim, "Truly, I tell you, this poor widow has put in more than all of them. For they all contributed out of their abundance, but she out of her poverty put in all she had to live on" (Luke 21:3-4 ESV)?

The question of significance and value is not one of size, status, and stature. That's what this account (albeit dramatized for effect) with the poor widow and Jesus reveals to us. It's deeper. It's more. It's worth digging into.

And it all starts with a question.

One question has sparked and inspired every word that follows in this book. If applied and asked with a humble and willing heart, this one question can forever alter how we view our lives, time, talents, dreams, callings, every day, and future.

Asking the Question

Is it too small a thing? This outwardly unassuming question is more than a string of six simple words. It's a question that pops up—if we're paying attention—in all areas of life. It'll tiptoe in as we're washing that sink full of dishes. It will sneak up on us as we pretend we don't see our neighbor as we back out of the driveway. It will plague us as we scroll through social media or try, yet again, to read our slightly dusty Bibles as we know we *should*.

It's a question that has been lurking and changing lives since the beginning of humanity's journey on Earth. The original packaging may have been different, but the meaning is the same. Do you remember that slippery serpent and the conversation he initiated with Eve in Genesis? He came spewing poisonous words, deceiving and distracting Eve from the truth of what God had already said.

"Did God actually say, 'You shall not eat of any tree in the garden?'" he questioned Eve (Genesis 3:1 ESV). *Did God really say?* To her credit, Eve stands up to the accusation and corrects him—kind of. "We may eat of the fruit of the trees in the garden, but God said, 'You shall not eat of the fruit of the tree that is in the midst of the garden, neither shall you touch it, lest you die,'" she responded (vs. 2-3). The touching and dying part was her addition.

Unfortunately, the serpent's cunning response convinced her God was holding back something better than all He had freely offered:

> But the serpent said to the woman, "You will not surely die. For God knows that when you eat of it, your eyes will be opened, and you will be like God, knowing good and evil." So when the woman saw that the tree was good for food, and that it was a delight to the eyes, and that the tree was to be desired to make one wise, she took of its fruit and ate, and she also gave some to her husband who was with her, and he ate (vs. 4-6 ESV).

Every other tree in the garden was theirs for eating, but the serpent shifted Eve's focus onto what she didn't have. That one tree. The one forbidden thing. *It couldn't be that bad, could it?*

Ultimately, the serpent convinced Eve it was too small a thing. What God had done, what He had put in front of them, and what

He was offering them was too small a thing. It wasn't enough.

Is it too small a thing? This question also appears *as is* in Scripture in the book of Numbers. Before we take a look, let's catch up on the story.

In the beginning... No, I'm just kidding. We don't have to go all the way back to Genesis. Let's fast forward to Moses, the notorious ten plagues, and the miraculous crossing of the Red Sea. The Israelites, God's chosen people, are finally free from 400 years of slavery and oppression in Egypt. God guides them through the wilderness toward the Promised Land. On their journey, God delivers them from hunger, enemies, and even their own mistakes time and time again. He shows Himself faithful, powerful, and worthy of honor, reverence, and praise.

While in the wilderness, God takes care of some critical family housekeeping, communicating primarily through Moses. God gives the Law—the Ten Commandments and more. He instructs His people to build the Tabernacle, or traveling dwelling place of His presence. He organizes and assigns tribes and their respective responsibilities. Essentially, God shapes them into a society with rules, boundaries, and ways of life determined according to His will.

In Numbers 16, a man named Korah and 250 followers approach Moses, their God-appointed leader, and ask for more than God had already given and entrusted to them. Korah is part of the tribe of Levi—most notable for being the tribe of priests. However, Korah is not a priest; he oversees the transportation of the holiest items. This isn't enough for him, however. He wants what Moses and Aaron, the High Priest and Moses's brother, have—the position, the recognition, the status.

IS IT TOO SMALL A THING

What is Moses's response? First, he falls on his face, approaching God with humility. Then, he delivers a speech, proclaiming that God will be the one to reveal who is right in this situation. It is at this moment that *the* question is asked:

> And Moses said to Korah, "Hear now, you sons of Levi: *is it too small a thing* for you that the God of Israel has separated you from the congregation of Israel, to bring you near to himself, to do service in the tabernacle of the LORD and to stand before the congregation to minister to them, and that he has brought you near him, and all your brothers the sons of Levi with you? And would you seek the priesthood also? Therefore it is against the LORD that you and all your company have gathered together (Numbers 16:8-11 ESV, emphasis added).

Is it too small a thing?

These men are chosen not just as Israelites but as part of the tribe of Levi. They are separated unto God and given special responsibilities and specific ministry for and to the people of God, The Levites enjoy a particular calling from God: *Only* the tribe of Levi is allowed anywhere near the Tabernacle, the presence of God. But it isn't enough for Korah and the other men. Moses perceives their motive and aptly asks the right question: *Is it too small a thing?*

So, what happens? The ground splits apart and swallows up Korah and a couple of other leaders of the coup, including their families. Fire consumes the remaining 250 men, but it doesn't stop there. The rest of the Israelites accuse Moses and Aaron of killing these men, and a plague comes upon the people. The plague only stops when Aaron walks into the crowd, not fearing for his health and safety, and makes atonement for them: "He stood between the dead and the living, and the plague was stopped" (Numbers 16:48

ESV). By the time the whole affair—Korah and his followers and the plague—is over, thousands of people have died.

Apparently, what God had done for them was too small a thing. It was too small a thing that He delivered them from slavery, provided food daily out of nothing, kept them safe and protected in the wilderness, and defeated their enemies. It was all too small. Not enough. They may not have said it with their mouths, but their actions, thoughts, complaints, and constant want for more said far more than their words ever could.

It's not wrong to approach God with our needs and even our wants. I don't even think it is wrong to ask for more. This account reveals, however, that the heart and motivation behind the requests matter. We can see how these men approached Moses and, ultimately, God with an attitude of entitlement and a lack of gratitude, and it didn't go well.

What About Us?

Is it too small a thing what He has done for *us*?

Is it too small a thing where He has brought us and how He has provided for us?

Is it too small a thing when our prayers are answered?

Is it too small a thing that Jesus paid the ultimate price to give us peace with God, providing a way back to Him?

Is it too small a thing _____ (fill in the blank)?

Maybe we aren't saying it with our words, but what about our actions? Our attitudes? Our thoughts?

Is it too small a thing? You may get tired of hearing this question by the time we reach the end of this book because we're going to look at it from different angles and various parts of our lives. The following pages are anchored by our new favorite question.

Is it too small a thing...
1. Who God is and what He has done?
2. What is in front of us?
3. What God is asking of us?

I hope that this question leaps from the black and white letters on this page to full-colored, vibrant, life-changing words nestled deep within our hearts. Because I'm seeing it happen in my own life, I'm convinced that this simple, unassuming question, embraced and applied, will bring us closer to God. We will begin cherishing the right now of our lives and fully living on mission for the glory of God and the good of His people.

But before we get to that, let's dig deep into who God is and what He has done for us. So, while this book is about the surprising significance of small things, we will start by exploring how big our God is. Maybe it'll feel like a hard turn, but this is where we must begin. God, and God alone, is our foundation, our point of origin, and He sets our perspective. He is our absolute.

To draw out small, seemingly singular stories in the Word of God that hold deeper, eternal meaning, I have also sprinkled in the accounts of four ordinary women in the Old Testament. We may already know their stories (or maybe they will be new to us), but I'm not sure we fully understand how relatable they are. Their stories of heartbreak, perceived insignificance, and questions come together as part of the beautiful tapestry of God's good and perfect plan for all of humanity. Through their stories, we will see how *small doesn't mean insignificant* and how the same can be said of our lives.

So, friend, if you're with me—if you're ready to move forward and do the hard and holy work of asking yourself over and over if it's too small a thing—then I invite you to approach this book with an open mind and heart. My pastor once said, "Honesty and humility lead to wide-open spaces of freedom." That is what will be required as you continue: honesty and humility. The result will be those wide-open spaces of freedom—freedom to fully live the life God has for you. Your significance and the significance of every little thing you do or don't do will no longer be in question.

Make This Prayer Yours

Heavenly Father, you are holy. You are not like me. I acknowledge and honor that. Lord, from the deepest part of my heart and soul, I thank you for who you are and what you have done for me. You do not owe me anything. Not a thing. Jesus is enough and will always be enough. Lord, I ask for your help keeping my perspective straight and true. Help me remember that what you have done for me is no small thing. Help me remember that all the things—big and small—are your goodness and grace. May my actions and heart never say it is too small a thing—that you are too small. I love you, and I'm so grateful. In the name of Jesus, amen.

Tamar's Story

Found in Genesis 38

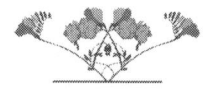

What about me?

I've been entirely forgotten.

I must be worthless.

I wonder if these thoughts plagued Tamar, a widow without children and without the agency of her own life, as she was relegated to a life of waiting—placed out of sight and out of mind.

After her first husband's death, her status as a childless widow put her at the mercy of her late husband's family, for she had no legal, economic, or social standing. Customary for ancient Near East culture, the next eldest brother was expected to perform his familial duty and produce an heir for his deceased brother. This child would have ensured Tamar's position within the family, albeit tenuous, while securing her dead husband's estate. However, what followed is nothing short of a soap opera—sex, drama, death, and a shocking twist of events.

The duty-bound brother-in-law took measures to guarantee he would not impregnate Tamar when they came together. He had no interest in producing and raising an heir for his dead brother. Unfortunately, his life was cut short, and Tamar was left, once again, without a child. Her father-in-law, Judah, sent Tamar back

TAMAR'S STORY

to her father's house to live as a widow and wait for her younger brother-in-law to grow up.

Years passed. Time ticked away. Tamar waited. And waited. And waited.

Eventually, Judah's young son had grown up, and yet Tamar waited. Still out of sight and out of mind. Forgotten. Unworthy of the now-grown son and the dignity he could provide for her through an heir—a child.

What about me?

I've been entirely forgotten.

I must be worthless.

Forgotten, feeling worthless, and without hope, Tamar's life had been reduced to that of a woman with no future unless it was given to her by one of the men in her life.

Like the modern woman she was not, Tamar decided to take matters into her own hands. One day, when she heard Judah was near her neck of the woods, she disguised herself as a prostitute and waited near the road. Judah approached this presumed prostitute and struck up a deal. She would sleep with him for the payment of a young goat, which he promised to deliver, and even pledged his seal, cord, and staff until the goat was received.

It was an age-old story of lust and deception—one that finds itself at the heart of the story of God's people time and time again.

As a result, Tamar finally conceived. When Judah learned of her indiscretion—for she was a widow and her behavior merited severe punishment—he sought her death, having no idea *he* was the father.

In spectacular and dramatic fashion, Tamar revealed the father's identity as the owner of the seal, cord, and staff she had in her possession. It was a plot twist Judah didn't see coming. In the end, he admitted his wrongdoing in not giving Tamar to his youngest son. Tamar now had a future and standing within the family and soon gave birth to twins.

But her story doesn't stop there…

Part 1

Is It Too Small a Thing...
Who God is and What He has Done?

In this first section of the book, we will focus on laying the foundation upon which we will build. Before we can look at our own lives, personally and missionally, we must understand our place and our position. That only rightfully happens when we put our focus and attention on God.

In this section, we will deepen our understanding of the following:

- Who God is
- What He has done
- The hope we have because of Him

The purpose of this part of the book is to provide the proper perspective we need before moving forward. When this aligning perspective is not accurate, it shows up in the rest of our lives. It shows up in how we live, view the life we have been given, and even treat others. It shows up in the significance we ascribe to every little thing. This is where we have to start.

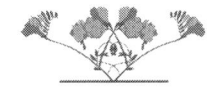

Chapter 2
Big God

"Look at all those people down there. They look like little bitty ants," my innocent, high-pitched 5-year-old voice squeaked in amazement.

While the details of this memory are fuzzy, I do remember watching teeny tiny people park their appropriately minuscule cars in the grid-like parking spots from the smudged window of a cold, sterile doctor's office. The ground below was full of movement and people going about their lives. They didn't know a bored and curious child had her face pressed against a window, watching from quite a few stories above them.

I remember wondering if this was what we looked like to God—busy little ants going about our business far, far below Him. Does He enjoy watching the patterns we make with our parking and driving? Does He try to count how many people enter and exit the building? Does He even notice *me* at all? This memory fragment is embedded in my mind because it was the first time I imagined how big God must be and was overcome by how small

I truly am.

How Big is God?

God is big. We all nod our heads to that and acknowledge it as true. As Christians, we serve a big God, but when was the last time we sat with those three words?

God. Is. Big.

What exactly does that mean?

It's vague and imprecise wording. Sometimes our teenage boys have *big* appetites. Sometimes we have a *big* meeting that causes us a *big* amount of anxiety. Sometimes there is a *big* family fight that leads to years of resentment. Big is relative and constantly changing to fit into whatever circumstance we decide to apply it.

Okay, so how big *is* God? Well, that's a tricky question. He cannot be measured because He has no beginning and no end. He always was, always is, and always will be. He is infinite. Truly immeasurable. However, while He, the limitless One, cannot be measured, we *can* attempt to be more precise and more descriptive with our language concerning His immeasurable size. Thankfully, we can grow in our understanding of just how vast He is.

This is my feeble attempt to expand our comprehension of the extensive boundlessness of our God.

I homeschooled my three children for precisely one school year. We learned about the ocean, fractions, writing essays...and how limited I am with my patience and kindness—all essential things to know. But the one thing that has refused to leave my thoughts—that has irrevocably shaped my view of God—is just how expansive the universe is. What we can view in the sky above with our naked eyes is barely a speck of what is up there.

BIG GOD

We live in a sleepy, rural town surrounded by rolling fields of grazing cattle, sprawling ranches, and dusty roads traveled by countless pickup trucks. Out here, the sky seems endless; it just goes on and on. While the landscape remains the same, only changing with the seasons, the masterpiece above is something new to behold every day. The cotton candy colors of the sunrises rival only the fiery, burning tones of the sunsets. Once the sun finally descends, however, the real show begins. The stars come out to play and don't hold anything back.

When we look up at the night sky and admire all the twinkling stars, it's easy to undervalue the magnitude of what we are beholding. Those brilliant shining lights are trillions and trillions of miles away. The sun is the closest star to us; the next nearest is approximately twenty-five trillion miles further away! According to the homeschool curriculum we used, it's estimated that there are about one hundred billion galaxies in the universe, and each galaxy contains an average of two hundred billion stars. That calculates to be 20,000,000,000,000,000,000,000 (that's twenty-two zeroes!) stars in the universe![1]

That number is entirely out of our mental grasp! Our minds simply respond, "Wow! That's a lot!" Isn't that what you thought when you saw all those zeroes? Let's stop for a minute, however, and try to put a handle on these numbers.

Recently, I googled how long it would take a person to count to one billion. While I came across varying answers—some thoughtful, some pure guesses, and some mathematically supported—the consensus is that it would take a very, very long time.

If it were possible to say one number per second, a person, in theory, could reach one billion in just under thirty-two years.[2]

Now, that would only happen if said counter did nothing else for those thirty-two years while perfectly speaking the numbers in exactly one-second intervals—no pausing for breath or taking a much-needed drink of water.

What happens when she gets to those eight and nine-digit numbers, however? Is it even possible to say one hundred thirty-two million four hundred fifty-six thousand seven hundred sixty-seven in one single second and immediately follow it up with the next nine-digit number?

While the initial answer of about thirty-two years seems plausible, it is actually quite a low estimate. Using a more accurate *average* of seconds per number and considering the necessity of breathing, resting, and other bodily functions, it could take somewhere around two hundred fifty years for a single person to count to one billion![3] In other words, it is not humanly possible.

Now, let's bring it back to the stars. Don't forget we are talking about trillions, not a single billion. In fact, there are *one thousand billion* in one trillion! The next closest star to us here on Earth, other than the sun, is twenty-five trillion miles away. That's *one thousand billion times twenty-five* miles to only the next star! What conclusion does that bring us to? The universe is mind-bending, astronomically enormous, gigantic, humongous, massive—I don't even know the appropriate term to use.

The universe is utterly expansive, and God created it all. That's what Genesis 1:1 tells us. This is the first thing we learn about God; it is the very first sentence in the Bible. He made all of it—everything we see and everything we couldn't possibly see. It wasn't a mistake, a fluke, or an accident. God is the Grand Architect, the Master Creator. And the Creator cannot be outmatched, outdone, or outgrown by His creation. It just isn't possible. Our God is bigger.

God. Is. Big.

Wrestling with the Bigness God

My grandfather was a hobbyist woodworker. I have some wooden toys, a step stool, and a few other odds and ends etched with his name. There is one wooden item, unlike the rest, however. It's rudimentary and, honestly, seems unfinished and unskilled. From what I can tell, it's supposed to be a bird whittled down from what might have been a tree branch. When I think about the patience and the time it must have taken to render the smooth, yet oddly shaped, bird—carefully shaving and carving bit by bit—I wonder if he was pleased by what took shape.

The art of whittling is not a skill I'm particularly interested in developing—at least, not intentionally. But I'm guilty—and so are you—of "whittling" something or even some people more often than I care to admit.

As a parent, I have often disappointed my children's high hopes, shrinking them considerably. Or unfortunately, there have been times when I cut down their self-esteem by not believing they could achieve a particular goal or outcome.

How many times have I thrown a snarky comment toward my husband that, I later found out, deflated his confidence?

What about confining a friend, neighbor, or even a stranger into a preconceived idea of who I think she is or what I think she could accomplish?

And then, of course, we constantly whittle *ourselves* down to size, boxing ourselves into a pre-fashioned idea of what we must be or do. We're guilty of holding even ourselves back, often shrinking back in fear, from what God may have intended for us or may be asking of us.

This innate tendency to confine and conform people, our lives, and practically everything around us also reaches in vain toward our big, limitless, immeasurable God. We prefer to measure things, understand them, and know what we are working with. So, it's only natural for that same inclination to be directed toward God, whom we cannot measure or come to a full working knowledge of. After all, his ways and thoughts are higher than ours, "just as the heavens are higher than the earth" (Isaiah 55:9 ESV).

The late Eugene Peterson poses a question in his book, *A Long Obedience in the Same Direction*, that, in my opinion, should be wrestled with openly and honestly when it comes to the grandeur of God:

> Will we let God be as He is, majestic and holy, vast and wondrous, or will we always be trying to whittle Him down to the size of our small minds, insist on confining Him within the boundaries we are comfortable with, refuse to think of Him other than in images that are convenient to our lifestyle?[4]

Will we let Him be as He is—in our lives and minds? Obviously, we can't restrict Him in reality, but we can limit how we perceive Him and work with Him and what we are willing to give Him. Confining Him in our lives doesn't hurt *Him*; it only hurts us. It limits us. It confines us. When we try to whittle Him down to whatever shape or size we are comfortable with, we end up whittling ourselves instead.

There's a beautiful picture painted for us within Scripture of God being the potter and us the clay, shaped and molded by His deft, careful, caring hands (Isaiah 64:8). He's not an amateur like my grandfather, simply searching for a hobby to fill his time. Nor is He whittling us down to size, shrinking who we are. Instead, He works us, uses what He will, and forms us into what He has intended all along. We become more than mere art projects. We become His masterpieces, His chosen works of art (Ephesians 2:10).

Will we let Him be as He is? Will we let Him do what He will in our lives?

Better Than Big

One of A. W. Tozer's most frequently quoted declarations is appropriate to bring into this conversation. He says, "What comes into our minds when we think about God is the most important thing about us."[5] We can't leave this topic only having addressed the vastness of God. If that is all we know about Him or what we think about the most, then we are in danger of living according to false assumptions about Him. If only His size pops into our minds when we think about God, pray to Him, or talk about Him, then we've effectively put Him in a box—an extraordinarily-sized box, but a box all the same.

We would be in danger of viewing God as just *the Big Guy upstairs*. Or, maybe, we would expect Him to be aloof, unaware, unconcerned about us *all the way down here*—much like how I felt as a young girl, wondering if God even noticed my tiny self. Because He is our infinite God, we might start thinking He's too big for us. Maybe He's just too big to notice or care.

God is better than just big, though; He is also close! He is immeasurable and infinite—more extensive than we could ever hope to grasp—but He is not distant. He is not *the big guy upstairs*, waiting to crack down when we make a mistake. He is not reclining in His heavenly La-Z-boy, chomping on popcorn and watching our lives like an afternoon soap opera. He is neither hands-off nor a puppeteer obsessed with control of the story. No! Throughout the whole narrative of the Bible, we see a big God who continues to draw near to His people (which we will address further in the next chapter).

In Psalm 8, David explores this mystery of a vast yet close God. He famously writes, "When I look at the night sky and see the work of Your fingers—the moon and the stars You set in place—what is man that You should think of him, the son of man that You should care for him?" (vs. 3-4 NLT).

Our God is not only *big* enough, *mighty* enough, and *creative* enough to make all that we see in the night sky (and all that we don't see), but He is also *close* enough to be mindful of us. He not only put all the trillions and trillions of stars in the sky into perfect placement, but He carefully and lovingly formed each of us, placing unique talents, desires, and purposes within us (Psalm 139). He is *close* enough to care about all the details of our lives (Psalm 37:23 NLT). He is *close* enough to bend down and hear our prayers (Psalm 116:2). He is *close* to the broken-hearted, the weary, and the sorrowful (Psalm 34:18).

Our infinite God is intimately close.

Discovering God as Close

Growing up as a pastor's kid, I have no memories of a time when I didn't believe in God. I don't have a dramatic before and after testimony of how I came to know Christ as Lord. I'm thankful for growing up as I did. I had a firmly rooted grasp on the reality of God, understanding that He has His hands in everything. As much as I could as a kid, I understood He was big—bigger than

I could imagine. It wasn't a stretch of my faith to believe He was in control and working to bring everything together *eventually* as only a big God could.

Like most Christian kids who grew up similarly to me, there came a time when knowing God as big and capable was not enough. And, again, as with most kids, that time came when I began stretching my wings to fly the coop—when I ventured off to college and beyond. Those few years were more formative to my faith than any years before, and they even rival any years since. Rather than being marked by mountaintops of success, achievements, and growth, these pivotal years were marked by the lowest valleys of death, struggles, and continual failure.

I set out for college far from home with high hopes, convinced I was called for somewhere greater than my hometown. I quickly learned that my self-assessment was out of touch with reality. I struggled to make friends, and I wrestled with debilitating homesickness. All the while, two of my aunts were diagnosed with cancer. They were fighting for their lives as I fought my inadequacy at living my own life. Needless to say, failure number one was abandoning college at the end of my first semester.

Returning home, ego bruised, I found myself at a loss for my next steps. Never had I been face-to-face with failure like that. I faltered longer than I'd like to admit, failing at another opportunity presented to me. Finally, after months of confusion, I worked up enough courage to step out on a new journey, attempting to follow God's lead. A ministry internship for young adults beckoned me north toward the tundra of Minnesota. My hopeful, 19-year-old heart *believed* my wandering would find meaning in this path forward. And, yet, days before I left, death had its first sting—the first of three in just over a year.

My aunt died of breast cancer, leaving a husband and three children at home. It devastated my family. We had prayed and believed for healing, trusting God heard us. It was the first time I remember thinking God didn't answer our prayers, but somehow, it didn't rock my faith in Him. I still believed Him to be who He said He was. Looking back, I'm convinced God held me tightly, refusing to let me go.

If you were to have asked me back then what I thought about God, I probably would have said He was good and kind and big—big enough to love all of us. All true. But it was during this time of dealing with the loss of my aunt while joining the ministry internship that I experienced His personal love for me. I was overwhelmed by His nearness.

Unbeknownst to me, the first week of the internship was a time called "Bootcamp." And it was precisely what you would imagine by the name. I hated every minute of it. I walked with a limp for weeks afterward. Looking back, I'm not sure it was legal. The purpose of this week was to encourage a fast-grown unity and teamwork mentality among all the interns. Well, it worked.

Amidst all the physical pain, I became more aware of God's presence. Every time I was in tears, a butterfly would fly by—just one. Every time I wanted to give up, there came the butterfly. Call it a coincidence, but I finally understood that God isn't just big and in control. I experienced Him as close—closer than I ever thought.

You see, my aunt loved butterflies and gardens; she even cultivated a butterfly garden in her kids' elementary school courtyard. She tended to it religiously; it is now dedicated to her memory. Butterflies were special when she was alive, but they took on a new significance to her children, our family, and me after she died.

I didn't know then, but this was just the beginning of the valleys. My grandfather passed away from cancer just six months later. My now husband and I began a forbidden relationship during the internship. We were subsequently removed from said internship just six weeks before we were set to graduate—another failure. A failure for which I, personally, was blamed by our leadership, and that haunted me for years. After all of this heartache, another aunt, who was like a second mother to me, died just a couple of weeks after the first anniversary of her sister's death—three deaths in my family from cancer in just over a year.

Why did this happen if God is big and nothing is impossible for Him?

Why wasn't He big in these situations?

I wrestled with those questions after the final death. This is not a book about why bad things happen. It's not a book meant to explore the inscrutable workings of God. This book is about a big God who makes a big deal about the small things in life. This book is about an infinite God intimately concerned with us as His people. So, while I asked those questions, God continued to pull me closer to Him. I don't know why I didn't give up other than because He wouldn't let me.

You can't convince me that God isn't a close God. You can't convince me He doesn't come near to the broken-hearted—that He doesn't see every tear we cry or hear every word we can barely utter in our agony.

In our pain, struggle, and failures, it's not just a big God that we need. We need a close God. God is big, yes. But because He is undeniably good, we can trust that He is also near.

Is It Too Small a Thing?

Is it too small a thing who God is? The way we live, the struggles and problems we face—are we afraid or reluctant to trust God with them? Is God too small to carry our burdens, the weights we insist on shouldering ourselves? Is He too distant to care? Maybe He doesn't notice our little ant-sized problems from His recliner far above.

No!

Because God is big but even better than big…because God is big AND close, we can trust Him to see, know, and care. We can confidently approach Him with our pain and struggles. We can cast our cares to Him and give Him our burdens. However, we won't have to cast them very far because He is as close as our very next breath.

God's infinite size means He has an endless capacity for everything we could ever need and everything we could ever cast to Him. His love for us is infinite in capacity *and* intimate in proximity.

Big is good, but big and close is even better.

Make This Prayer Yours

Who am I, Lord, that you would be mindful of me? Help me always to be thankful and in awe of who you are—how big and close you are. I don't deserve you. Lord, help me live my life in such a way that not only pleases you but praises you, magnifies you, and brings others into adoration of you. You are worthy of so much more than I can give, but I am grateful to be able to offer you what I have—to give you my life. May your praise ever be on my lips and in my heart. In the name of Jesus, amen.

Notes

1. Debbie and Richard Lawrence, *Our Universe* (Petersburg, KY: Answers in Genesis, 2016), 33, 35.

2. "How Long Does It Take to Count to a Billion?" Reference, last modified April 7, 2020, https://www.reference.com/world-view/long-count-billion-c1f1fc3ab57aebb.

3. Karl Smallwood, "How Long Would It Take to Count to a Billion and What's the Highest Anyone Has Counted?" Today I Found Out, May 11, 2017, https://www.todayifoundout.com/index.php/2017/05/long-take-count-billion/.

4. Eugene H. Peterson, *A Long Obedience in the Same Direction: Discipleship in an Instant Society* (Downers Grove, IL: IVP Books, 2000), 120.

5. A. W. Tozer, *The Knowledge of the Holy* (New York: HarperOne, 1978), 1.

Chapter 3
Big Plan

"Wait…this is one long story?" I marveled about the Bible more times than I could count during my internship in Minnesota.

Most of my time was spent in a classroom where our teacher, newly graduated from Bible college, walked us through the grand story of the Bible, book by book. As he began breaking down each book, showing us the arc of the story and the major themes, I was continually shocked by what I didn't know.

I knew Jesus, of course. I knew the classic Bible stories—Adam and Eve, Noah's ark, Samson, David and Goliath, among many others—but I merely understood them as separate, individual stories. The puzzle pieces were being put together for the first time, and I was amazed at the picture being revealed.

As someone who had been in church her whole life, I finally began to realize how beautiful, intricate, and hopeful the Bible truly is. I had never connected the stories from the Old Testament to the life-giving revelations of the New Testament. I didn't know God deliberately unveiled His big story—the one we're still a part of today—through the means of individuals and their respective stories.

However, the biggest revelation was that Jesus isn't only present in the New Testament. When Mary lovingly swaddled Him in rags and laid Him down in the manger, it was the first time Jesus—divine and holy—donned human flesh, but it was not the beginning of Jesus' work here on Earth. I discovered breadcrumbs of His existence throughout the seemingly disjointed stories of the Old Testament. My eyes began looking for Him on every page. With a newfound awe of the Word of God, I came to know my God not only as a big God but as a big God with a big plan to redeem His people by coming closer than we could ever deserve.

In this chapter, we will look at God's paramount plan, which He is still working out today. The whole story of the Bible—the metanarrative of Scripture—is this grand master plan. When we do the work of learning how it all fits together and recognize that we are a part of His marvelous story, I believe our only natural response will be our wholehearted devotion to follow Him. And in that, we'll be encouraged to trust Him with even the smallest things because the biggest thing has already been accomplished.

The What and the Why

My husband once said in a sermon, "Only a big God could do what He did, but only a close God would." God's sovereignty, omniscience, and transcendence—theological words used to describe the divine aspects of His nature—make it *possible* for Him to act in such a marvelous way. It's His immanence, His nearness, and His everlasting love, however, that make it *impossible* for Him to not. Because He is big and close, the most beautiful, life-giving story ever told is a reality we still live out today. It's our story, and God—the Father, the Son, and the Holy Spirit—is our hero.

BIG PLAN

What exactly did He do, and why did He do it?

To answer, let's go back to Sunday School for a few minutes. Having a firm grasp on the *whole* story from the beginning to now (because it's still in progress) is essential to understanding the what and the why.

God created the heavens and the earth out of nothing. Remember all those stars we attempted to number? God put them there. He brought function and purpose to everything we see on this earth—the plants, the water, the animals, and even people.

Out of the dust, God made Adam and breathed His life-giving breath into him. God, then, formed Eve from the side of Adam. This first couple had it all. They lived in paradise, enjoying perfect communion with God and each other. They dwelled in the perfect purpose and presence of God. And, yet, before long, they chose something else. They chose their own way, their own path. They sinned against their Creator by eating of the one tree forbidden to them, by disobeying God's command (Genesis 1-3). That choice and their sin put into motion the reality we are still experiencing thousands of years later.

Remember that theological word I pulled out a minute ago? *Omniscience*. It is a characteristic of God that belongs to only Him; He alone is all-knowing. He cannot be surprised; there is nothing He does not know—yesterday, today, and tomorrow. As finite beings, it is difficult to comprehend that God is unbound by time and place. He is not limited in knowledge and understanding as we are.

So, just in case we are tempted to think otherwise, God was not caught unaware. He was not surprised by Adam and Eve's actions. He already had a plan, and He was ready to execute it.

Adam and Eve lost God's perfect presence for all of us, but God was committed to restoring us. He had already decided to redeem us.

From the very beginning, Jesus was the plan for our redemption, but God took it slowly. He built the plot, crafted the story, and, ultimately, taught His people *who* He is through every piece of it. With Noah and Abraham, He began shaping their understanding of a God who is almighty, everlasting, and involved in the big picture, but also of a God who sees and will provide in the here and now.

Significantly, Abraham became the father of a nation of people to whom God chose to reveal Himself—to lead, guide, and love—in order to show all of humanity who He is. For most of the Old Testament, God's bigger story zeroed in on this distinct and set apart group of people, the nation of Israel.

Moses became a central character—a foreshadowing of *the* central character, Jesus. God showed Himself to Moses through a burning bush and announced His name as Yahweh, further revealing Him as a personal God (Exodus 3). Through Moses, God delivered His people from slavery in Egypt. Miracle after miracle proved His unquestioned, unrivaled power. Everything they experienced emphasized this truth: He is who He says He is. Their deliverance from Egypt became the ultimate example of God's master plan—the undisputed, undeniable proof that the story He was writing was good and beautiful. Time and time again, God pointed back to what He did in Egypt; He asked them to remember His faithfulness. Time and time again, however, the people forgot, took it for granted, or didn't seem to care.

Eventually, God gave His people His Law, outlining how they were to live in light of who He is. No one could measure up,

BIG PLAN

however. No one could fulfill it or follow it perfectly. Through a system of sacrifices and the priesthood, God provided a way for the people to come to Him, although imperfectly and with limits. God was clear about the requirements—that they were to live their lives with hearts turned toward Him.

For hundreds of years, God's people followed a pattern. They turned to Him for a time, and then they ran away, shifting their hearts and lives toward other gods and idols. God spoke through His prophets, imploring them to return to Him, promising that the impending judgment would be appeased. He sent warning after warning, yet their hearts continued to harden. Their eyes continued to wander.

For centuries, God waited patiently. He called out and offered mercy. His arms were outstretched and ready for them to return at any moment. Judgment and destruction were inevitable, however, because they didn't listen. They didn't turn back to God.

Enemy nations conquered all of Israel over a period of years. This was the judgment and destruction that could have been avoided. God offered mercy, but His people never wholeheartedly reached out for it. They lost their kingdom. They lost their land. And many lost their way. Israel as a nation never returned to what it once had been.

Around 400 years later, a baby was born. This baby was the answer. He was the plan made flesh. Since the beginning, God had planted seeds of this baby's coming. He planted seeds of our need for the man the baby grows to become. No one could fulfill the Law. No one could right the wrong of Adam and Eve. No one could live in such a way that would bring God's people back to Him…until this baby was born.

Until Jesus.

Jesus became our way back to God by fulfilling all the requirements. He did what we could not and could never do—He "offered Himself to God as a perfect sacrifice for our sins" (Hebrews 9:14 NLT).

All God and all man, Jesus is the only answer. He is the plan, the only way. Jesus Himself even declares, "I am the way, and the truth, and the life. No one comes to the Father except through me" (John 14:6 ESV). He lived. He died (as an innocent man), but He did not stay dead! He lived again. He ascended to Heaven, where He currently sits at the right hand of the Father. He is now the One who goes between us, *the imperfect,* and God, *the perfect.* He is the bridge. He gives us access through the Holy Spirit to once again live with purpose in His presence.

But, it is not yet perfect. It is not yet complete. Just like we are waiting for that great and glorious day of completion, we will have to wait until the next chapter to dig deeper into what is still promised to come.

Now, though, we can address the what and the why with a solid footing, having a grasp on the fundamentals of the big story.

What did God do, and why did He do it?

Actually, the most straightforward answer I can give you might already be something you know by heart—a verse you probably have memorized and have heard too many times to count. It may have even lost its depth of meaning because of that familiarity. "For God so loved the world that He gave His only Son, that whoever believes in Him should not perish but have eternal life" (John 3:16 ESV).

What did He do?

God gave His Son, our Savior—Jesus Christ—as our perfect sacrifice, willing Him to be and do what we could not.

Why did He do it?

Because of His love for us.

Our big, expansive, infinite God came intimately close in the body of Jesus Christ and died for us to pave the way back to Him permanently. And this life-altering, life-redeeming act was spurred on and motivated by His love for us—His desire for communion and relationship with those He created.

On a Hill He Created

If you permit me, I want to camp here for a minute. I don't want to take for granted that we understand how monumental this one act by one (divine) man truly was. We hear it at church. We sing about it often. We tell our kids the story. Sometimes, we even tell others about it. But, do we sit with it, meditating on it, taking in the astounding implications presented by it?

Let's draw on what we learned in the previous chapter. All those trillions of stars—not to mention planets, moons, and any other celestial objects out there—were created by God. The whole of the universe was birthed according to His word. He made it all; He is the source of it all. And yet, He came down to dwell among it. To breathe the same oxygen His creation breathes. To walk the same dusty paths His creation walks. To die just as all creation dies.

Through sneers of derision from the people He came to save,

Jesus trudged forward on a hill He created. Beaten and bruised, He carried the burden of the cross and the burden of our sin on a hill He created. Gasping for breath, His body battled unimaginable pain, and His soul anguished the loss of His eternal communion with the Father on a hill He created. He gave it all—His life, His blood, His relationship with the Father—on a hill He created. The One who made it all, had it all, and is the source of it all, gave it all for you. For me.

How many times do we read about the mountains bowing before the Lord in the Psalms? Or the oceans roaring His praises? Psalm 148 is full of beautiful, poetic imagery of the stars, fire and hail, mountains and hills, trees, and all creeping things being encouraged to praise Him. All creation was made by Him and for Him, pointing to and revealing His "eternal power and divine nature" (Romans 1:20 ESV).

And yet, on the cross, Jesus is brought low before creation in His death. But thank God (literally) that it was Jesus's death on the cross—this very low moment—that led to Him being "highly exalted" by the Father (Philippians 2:8-9 ESV). His lowest point became the highest cause of praise for those who follow Him.

This was the plan. The only plan. The plan for our redemption. And it has been intricately crafted from the beginning of time. It's incomparable in scope, depth, and longevity because its author is utterly incomparable Himself.

Glimpses of Jesus

To entice your curiosity about God's big, beautiful plan from the beginning of time, I thought I would include a quick, definitely not exhaustive, list of foreshadows of Jesus found in the Old Testament. I call these "glimpses of Jesus"—little sneak peeks of

BIG PLAN

our promised Savior.

- The very first hint of our need for a Savior, and the promise of His coming, is found in God's reaction to the serpent and Adam and Eve's betrayal. To the serpent, God says, "I will put enmity between you and the woman, and between your offspring and her offspring; he shall bruise your head, and you shall bruise his heel" (Genesis 3:15 ESV).
- There are many glimpses of Jesus in the account of Abraham found in Genesis. One, however, stands out among the rest. When God asks Abraham to willingly sacrifice his son, Isaac, we get a preview of Jesus's sacrifice on the cross. More than that, though, God provides a substitute, a ram, to take the place of Isaac on the altar—just as Jesus is the substitute for us and our sins. (Genesis 22)
- In many ways, Moses is a compelling foreshadow of our Eternal Deliverer and High Priest. God uses Moses to deliver His people from Egypt and slavery—a picture of mankind's deliverance, found in Jesus, from the ways of this world and slavery to sin. God gives Moses the Ten Commandments and many other laws while on the mountain—a prelude to Jesus proclaiming the Law in a new, more profound way also on a mountain (the Sermon on the Mount, Matthew 5-7). Moses acts as the mediator between God and the people, and Jesus is now our mediator, who provides an even better way to God (Hebrews 10:19-22).
- In all the requirements of the Law—primarily found in Leviticus and Deuteronomy—we discover humanity's inadequacy to fulfill them. No one could. No one did. In that inadequacy, we also rediscover our need for a Savior. All the Laws point to our need for Jesus.

- Before the institution of kings in Israel, God works through people called judges. The judges call the people back to God after extended periods of waywardness and truly evil living. These judges are tiny peeks into the eternally saving work of Jesus.

- In Isaiah 49, a prophecy about the Lord's Servant—the coming Messiah—it is said:

    It is too small a thing for you to be my servant to restore the tribes of Jacob and bring back those of Israel I have kept. I will also make you a light for the Gentiles, that my salvation may reach to the ends of the earth (v. 6 NIV, emphasis added).

    Here, we see that the coming Messiah is meant to save all people groups—that His mission is not as small as the Israelites generally thought. And we now know Jesus fulfilled this: He came to seek and save all who are lost. What good news this is!

- In Micah, there is a prophecy of Jesus concerning His small and seemingly insignificant origins, the place of His birth: "But you, Bethlehem Ephrathah, though you are small among the clans of Judah, out of you will come for me one who will be ruler over Israel, whose origins are from of old, from ancient times" (v. 2 NIV).

    Bethlehem, we now know, is the birthplace of Jesus Christ. This ruler of ancient times "will be born in Bethlehem!"

- Psalm 23, the beloved psalm about our Lord and Shepherd, gives us a glimpse of Jesus as the Good Shepherd (John 10).

These foreshadows and glimpses of Jesus are some of the easier ones to recognize. Not much digging is required to make the connections. However, we could sit and study all day, every day and continue finding more dots to connect to our Savior. That is the beauty of Scripture. It all points to, reveals, and glorifies our King!

The way God constructed Scripture, the way He weaved every detail together, further reveals just how intricate, yet monumental, His plan truly is. God's plan far surpasses anything we could ever imagine, ask, or even think to ask. It was good for the people of the Old and New Testament, and it remains good for us today!

Big Plan, Long Game

If I had to choose my preferred type of movie or TV show, it would be one with a well-planned, meticulous story. I revel in plot development from the start. I look for clues along the way, hanging on to every word, wondering if it's something I'll need to remember in a few episodes. I want to be assured that a long, fulfilling story is being told from beginning to end. I'm even open to being surprised by the outcome *if* it is executed well. If I commit my time to watching something, I want it to be committed to me...or at least the idea of me. Playing the long game—that's what I want from my entertainment.

This is a compelling way to describe what we have discussed in this chapter. God has a big plan, and He's playing the long game with it. And He is really, really good at it. Think about how patient, determined, and committed He has been toward us—all of us. We see it clearly with the Israelites, but sometimes we struggle to see it here and now in our little stories.

Yes, God is still playing the long game! He is still patiently weaving the threads together, crafting this wonderful story with more intricacy and details than we imagine. And surprises? Oh, there have been plenty of those along the way. The Israelites could attest to that! And I think it's reasonable to expect plenty more to come.

God's proficiency at playing the long game has significant implications for our lives *right now*—not just our eternal future. How often do we feel ashamed when we mess up yet again? When we just can't seem to live out that truth our pastor keeps preaching? When we cover up a sin? When we yell at our kids again? When we make that choice we know we shouldn't have?

We have a timeline that we are convinced our lives should follow. We assume we should be at "stage five" when God is still working some things out in us at "stage two." When we make a course correction in life, we think God must be flabbergasted or at least annoyed. Shouldn't we already know how to hear from Him clearly by now? Shouldn't we be past this already?

Shouldn't we *this*…

Shouldn't we *that*…

I will say it again: God is playing the long game! Not just in the grand scheme of things, but He is playing the long game in your life, too. That timeline you have taped up in the control room of your mind? That's *your* timeline. Those lists of "shoulds" that seem just out of your reach? Those are *your* "shoulds."

Another way to say it is that God is a God of grace. He is a God of unfailing, long-suffering, patient, and merciful love. He knows and sees where the end is. He knows where He is taking you and how He is shaping you. He sees the bumps, bruises, hiccups, and outright sins in your life, and He is still there. With open arms, He is still there.

If He—the God of the universe, the beginning and end of all things—can offer you grace and mercy in the face of your shortcomings and failures, then can't you do the same thing?

Can you offer yourself grace when you feel lost?

Can you try to see yourself through His eyes when you fight against self-hatred?

Can you be kind to yourself even though you can barely see through the fog of failure, fear, and doubt?

We Don't Deserve It

All the personal failures and setbacks I experienced in my early adulthood happened during one of the most sensitive and impressionable times of life for anyone. Those years are formative for most of us. Rather than experiencing moments of personal achievement, or at the very least some sort of movement forward, I floundered and flailed.

Over time, I began to see myself as a failure, to think of myself as a failure.

Those individual bumps in the road somehow became my identity. I *was* a failure. *How could I ever expect to finish anything, accomplish any goals, or make anything of myself? I guess I just don't have it in me.*

I didn't have the framework of God's big plan and His exceptional long-game capability deeply rooted in my mind and heart. I hadn't grown enough to grasp this defining quality. So much of my story unfolding throughout this book is the slow and gentle process by which God began showing and teaching me who He is and the plan He is continually working out.

To this day, one of the most freeing, revelatory thoughts about my big God is that He is playing the long game. He's playing the long game even in my life, and He is so good at it. He is so much better at it than I am for myself. He has more grace, love, and kindness for me than I often have for myself. I sure don't deserve it, but I sure do appreciate it.

We don't deserve it, friend, but I hope we appreciate it. I hope our lives show Him how much we appreciate it.

Is It Too Small a Thing?

Is it too small a thing what God has done? Is this lofty plan of His too small to reach into your life and change everything? God's patience and His undeserved kindness, are they not enough? Is it not really what you need?

NO!

I want to repeat that over and over. No. No. No. Jesus is more than enough. Jesus is exactly what you needed and still need and will need every day of your life. There is no other, and there is no different plan that could have fulfilled your every need.

God's great plan overshadows all your problems, failures, and hang-ups. In fact, it is the BEST news you can hear right now. It *is* the gospel—the Good News. The gospel doesn't merely save your seat in eternity with God. No, the gospel saves you today. The gospel offers you hope for today. Peace for today. Joy for today. Endurance for today. The gospel is what you need today.

It is no small thing what God has done for you—the life of Jesus being poured out for you. It is His love for you on display. It is His willingness to go big for you, even though you are tempted to see yourself as too small to matter. You are not too meager for the love of God! You are not too trivial for the blood of Jesus!

All those individual stories we read in the Old Testament are part of the whole story of God and His people. The small stories haven't stopped. We're still living them out. Every day. Every ordinary, regular day. We are part of His story. Since He is the One writing it, we can have confidence in Him as we attempt to follow Him faithfully. After all, He has proven Himself faithful to us without fail.

Make This Prayer Yours

> Lord, I am humbled by your big plan and the lengths you have gone for your people and even me. Your love is more than I can comprehend, but I want to spend the rest of my days trying to grasp it more fully. I'm sorry when I take for granted what you have done. I don't want to be focused on myself and my plans and, then lose sight of how much you have given for me. I want to be aware of your sacrifice in my daily life. I want to live in light of what was done for me. I know I cannot do it perfectly, but I am thankful you are here to help me. I desire to please you with my life. Lord, please guide me and help me. In the name of Jesus, amen.

Chapter 4
Big Hope

When I was ten years old, I was convinced I would be flying a car rather than driving it by the time I was sixteen. I was sure of it. All the pictures of the future in my mind were of what the Disney Channel and Nickelodeon had promised me: space stations people actually lived on *in space*, brightly-hued leotard-like jumpsuits, and fancy gadgets for communicating with people anywhere and everywhere. I, for one, am thankful the spandex-laden dress options never took off in popularity. And their communication predictions have more or less become a reality. Where are those flying cars, though?

For those born before the turn of the century, do you remember what most futuristic movies and TV shows *used* to be like? They were full of innovation and creativity—jet packs, flying vehicles, teleportation, and even those crazy and unrealistic leotard numbers. In a very literal sense, the colors were bright and happy, exuding a light-hearted and generally pleasant feeling. The future was something to anticipate with hope and excitement.

However, the entertainment offered for our consumption depicts a future full of zombies, cataclysmic weather events, asteroids, aliens, or worse. When was the last time you walked away encouraged after watching a movie set in the future? Our children are growing up in a generation that genuinely assumes everything will fall apart at some point in their lifetime. Whether we realize it or not, we are being conditioned to expect the worst for the future.

The Merriam-Webster Dictionary defines *dystopia* as "an imagined world or society in which people lead wretched, dehumanized, fearful lives."[1] The dystopian genre is outrageously popular, whether it's literature, movies, or TV shows. However, what once may have been thought of as an imagined future is quickly becoming our culture's *assumed* future.

What has happened to our hope?

Why are we so easily consumed by fear when we look ahead?

As Christians, hope should be one of our defining characteristics. The world's view of the future may be fear-filled and hopeless, but the Christian's view of the future should be hope-filled and fearless. When we look forward, we should be filled with unwavering hope. We should be unshakably, irrevocably optimistic!

In 2021, I had the privilege of sharing a message with our church about the necessity of hope rising within us. It's a vital message because if hope doesn't rise, the fear that is so prevalent in the world will. This is a topic that hasn't lost its fire within me. If anything, it has only intensified. As fear continues to grow in the world, our hope must rise!

There's a common saying: "Whatever you feed will grow." Well, that applies here, friend. Whatever we feed will grow. We have a choice. Are we going to feed the fear or feed the hope? Are we going to lean into the anxiety and worries of the world, or will we lean into the hope offered by our big God who came closer than we deserve to eradicate all fear?

We Know How the Story Ends

I don't like scary movies. Suspense and intrigue, yes. Horror? Absolutely not! I have my limits. For a few minutes, though, imagine you have persuaded me to sit down and watch your favorite scary movie with you. As I'm enduring all the fright-inducing scenes, my eyes barely peeking through my fingers, you laugh and joke. You are enjoying all my squirming. You aren't on the edge of your seat, and your heart rate is annoyingly stable. (I'll be honest. If this is you, I don't know if we could be friends.)

We are watching the same movie. It's scary and tense, but our reactions are entirely different. Why? Because you have already seen it! The tension, discomfort, and fear I am experiencing are nonexistent for you because you know how it ends. You are no longer dwelling in the unknown. You aren't wondering what is going to happen.

Guess what! We know how this epic story ends—the one that burst to life at the sound of its Author's voice and continues even to this day. On the final pages of the book of Revelation, we find the most incredible ending ever told. (To be clear: this is the *only* time it is permissible to skip to the end of any book.) The elderly Apostle John obediently records a vision he received of the final outcome (as far as we know) of the chronicle of humankind:

> Then I saw a new heaven and a new earth, for the old heaven and the old earth had disappeared. And the sea was also gone. And I saw the holy city, the new

Jerusalem, coming down from God out of heaven like a bride beautifully dressed for her husband. I heard a loud shout from the throne, saying, "Look, God's home is now among his people! He will live with them, and they will be his people. God himself will be with them. He will wipe every tear from their eyes, and there will be no more death or sorrow or crying or pain. All these things are gone forever." And the one sitting on the throne said, "Look, I am making everything new!" And then he said to me, "Write this down, for what I tell you is trustworthy and true." And he also said, "It is finished! I am the Alpha and the Omega—the Beginning and the End. To all who are thirsty I will give freely from the springs of the water of life. All who are victorious will inherit all these blessings, and I will be their God, and they will be my children. (Revelation 21:1-7 NLT)

This, my friend, is how the story ends. A new heaven. A new earth. Everything new! No death. No sorrow. No pain. No tears. This is our future. We don't have to wonder anymore.

Knowing what is ahead doesn't automatically fill us with hope, though. It eases the tension and helps us imagine a better future than what is portrayed in all those movies and TV shows. It sparks optimistic imagination, but that can falter when life gets tough. When all we understand and expect of the future is the removal of everything evil, painful, and contrary to our flourishing, we may live in anticipation of simply *feeling better*. And I'd argue that is not, in fact, our big hope.

What is our Big Hope?

Our hope is not what God will do for us. Our big hope is God Himself. Our ultimate hope is the remarkable reality that God—

our Creator, our Savior, our Protector, our Provider, the One who knows every cell of our bodies, every hair on our heads, and every thought in our minds, the One who loves us beyond our comprehension—will live with us. He will be with us, and we will be with Him. That's what the end of Revelation tells us! He is our future, the greatest hope ever imagined.

As we discussed in the previous chapter, Adam and Eve once dwelled in God's perfect presence and purpose. It was lost in one moment, with one act of disobedience. Thousands of years later, the possibility of once again dwelling in the perfect presence and purpose of God was made possible in one moment with one act of obedience. Jesus's sacrifice provided more for us than a pathway to heaven. It wasn't about giving us a one-way ticket out of our mess or the chaos of the world around us. Jesus's death on the cross and victorious resurrection provided a way—the *only* way—back to God Himself. Our goal, our prize, is being restored once again into the perfect presence and purpose of God, our loving and faithful Creator.

In his first letter to believers, Peter reveals our hope through the lens of Jesus's ultimate sacrifice. He declares we are "born again to living hope through the resurrection of Jesus Christ" (1 Peter 1:3 ESV). *Living hope*! A few verses later, he says of believers, "And you have placed your faith and hope in God because He raised Christ from the dead and gave Him great glory" (v. 21 NLT). Hope finds its life in the fact that Jesus Christ died but didn't remain dead! He is still alive today! That's why Peter can aptly call it *living hope*.

Not only does Peter define our hope as alive, but he sets it upon an "inheritance that is imperishable, undefiled, and unfading, kept in heaven" (1 Peter 1:4 ESV). A word often used in the Bible concerning the future and what is promised to the faithful is *inheritance*. Interestingly, in the Old Testament, when

God allotted parts of the Promised Land to the various tribes of Israel, the Levite tribe, the tribe from which all the priests hailed—remember Korah?—received no land as an inheritance. Multiple times, God revealed *Himself* as their inheritance and portion (Numbers 18:20; Deuteronomy 18:1-2; Joshua 13:33). We also see this same language in the Psalms. "Lord, you alone are my inheritance, my cup of blessing. You guard all that is mine" (Psalm 16:5 NLT).

Peter employs this rich history surrounding *inheritance* to make a startling point. He reveals that we, as members of God's family, are a "chosen people" and, in fact, "royal priests" (1 Peter 2:9 NLT). As His priests, our inheritance, just as it was in the days of the Old Testament, is our Almighty God! Since He is what we are looking forward to, of course, our hope cannot wither, fade, or change. Because He cannot wither, fade, or change! He is our imperishable inheritance. He is our unfading hope.

Unshakably optimistic. Unwaveringly hopeful. These countercultural descriptions can be said of us when we understand in whom our hope is placed. Grasping the gravity of our immeasurable God's epic plan produces in us formidable hope—hope that cannot be swayed because our God will not be swayed.

When Hope Feels Lost

Let's push the pause button because I can hear that question just barely niggling in the back of your mind. *But what if all hope feels lost?* Please, don't be ashamed to ask that question. Don't push it back down, afraid it's the wrong question or a sign of a lack of faith. God can handle it.

God can handle *all* of your questions. Have you ever noticed how many despairing questions with which the psalmists cry out to God?

- O Lord, why do you stand so far away? Why do you hide when I am in trouble? (Psalm 10:1 NLT)
- O Lord, how long will you forget me? Forever? How long will you look the other way? How long must I struggle with anguish in my soul, with sorrow in my heart every day? (Psalm 13:1-2 NLT)
- My God, my God, why have you abandoned me? Why are you so far away when I groan for help? Every day I call to you, my God, but you do not answer. Every night you hear my voice, but I find no relief. (Psalm 22:1-2 NLT)
- "O God my rock," I cry, "Why have you forgotten me? Why must I wander around in grief, oppressed by my enemies?" (Psalm 42:9 NLT)
- Did I keep my heart pure for nothing? Did I keep myself innocent for no reason? I get nothing but trouble all day long; every morning brings me pain. (Psalm 73:13-14 NLT)

These questions aren't a precursor to a lack of faith as long as they are directed to God with a heart yearning for Him, grappling to continue trusting Him. In each of these Psalms, the writers are unashamed in admitting their struggles, but they are just as dogged in their determination to persevere with hope. In Psalm 42, for example, the psalmist recalibrates his hopelessness—not just once, but twice! He concludes, "Why am I discouraged? Why is my heart so sad? I will put my hope in God! I will praise him again—my Savior and my God!" (vs. 5, 11 NLT). Asaph, the writer of Psalm 73, makes this grand statement *after* baring it all to God and seeking His presence, "My health may fail, and my spirit may grow weak, but God remains the strength of my heart;

he is mine forever" (v. 26 NLT). I could go on, but I think you get my point.

Ask your questions. Wrestle with God. Allow Him to draw you closer, even amid your pain and doubt.

When I think about losing hope, I can't help but think of Jesus's disciples and friends. The Gospels give us a small view of the three years of Jesus's earthly ministry. In John's Gospel, he tells us there aren't enough books in the world to write about all that Jesus did (John 21:25). What we know is only part. Yet, I think we would all agree that what the disciples experienced would have been the highest of mountaintops. They were with the Messiah, the Savior of the world. They personally knew the One who was born to change the whole world. Can you imagine how optimistic about the future they must have been?

As high as that pinnacle was, the depth of their shocking low must have been greater. Imagine what they thought and felt as Jesus was taken away in the garden. What was Peter thinking as he sat cowering and watching Him be beaten and ridiculed? Or, the women—they watched Jesus be crucified on the cross, one nail at a time. They witnessed His struggle for breath, his pain with every inhale and exhale, and his anguish as He cried out to the Father. As Jesus breathed His final breath, they probably held theirs.

Jesus died. The one who came to save them—their Messiah, the ruler they had been anticipating, the one Moses and the Prophets had spoken and written about—died. He was supposed to change things. He was supposed to free them. He was supposed to be *it*. Surely, He wasn't supposed to die. I can almost hear His followers crying in grief, "How could this be the plan? This isn't how it was supposed to go!"

Now, because we know the whole story, we know this wasn't the end. They didn't know that. To them, this was how it ended. To them, the cross was utter defeat. They had a good run and had gotten their hopes up, but this was it. All hope was lost.

Something happened to revive and fortify their hope, though. Just when they thought it was gone forever, their hope made a triumphant return. When Jesus rose from the dead, it wasn't just His body that was resurrected. Hope was resurrected, too! What once was lost was found again in Jesus's victory over death.

Friend, I don't know what may be causing you to question your hope. I don't know what you are facing right now—or what you have been up against in the past. But I do know who is right there with you in it. I know who has already paid the highest price, so you would never have to live without hope. I know who is holding you by your right hand, unwilling to let you go. I know who's got you.

Hebrews 10:23 encourages you to "hold fast the confession of our hope without wavering" (ESV). Hold fast. Cling to. Take full possession of. Do not let go. This exhortation to not let go of hope implies you can, in fact, let go. You can give up on it. You can stop holding onto hope. But I'm encouraging you just as the author of Hebrews encourages all of us, hold fast your hope! Refuse to let go.

The last part of that verse unlocks your ability to persevere. You can hold onto your hope because "he who promised is faithful." Your hope is anchored in His faithfulness. So, even in your despair, when all hope feels lost, know that He has not gone anywhere. More than anything, your eyes and heart need to be awakened again to His ever-enduring, unfailing presence in your life. The Living Hope Himself is for you, with you, and in you!

Hope for Today

Sometimes when we talk about hope, it's easy to focus on it being for someday. I tend to think that sells hope short. Here's how I see it: Hope looks forward to the future, trusting God *is* there. Hope also looks back into the past, remembering He *was* there. And hope provides help for today because we are confident He *is* here, even now. Hope isn't simply for someday. Hope is for today.

Of course, when we read the passage at the end of Revelation, we understand it is speaking of the future. But the hope we find there touches our lives today because of Jesus. Dallas Willard puts words to a question that needs to be addressed. He asks, "Does Jesus only enable me to 'make the cut' when I die? . . . It is good to know that when I die all will be well, but is there any good news for life?"[2] Yes, there is good news for life! Yes, what we know and trust about the future affects our right now, everyday lives.

Today, you can do the hard thing in front of you because you know He is with you.

Today, you can say no to that temptation lurking at the door because He is with you.

You can reach out to a hurting friend, unsure of your ability to help but confident in His ability to work through you.

You can take that step toward a dream long buried deep in your heart.

You can show up for your kids, give your best at work, and even pray for that neighbor who gets on your nerves.

Today, you can do what is right in front of you—whatever it is—because He is with you.

BIG HOPE

And one glorious, long-awaited day, our hope will be fulfilled in our Lord's physical presence with us. One day, we'll be with Him face-to-face and realize how much He has indeed done for us. This big hope is the fuel that keeps us going, that keeps us looking ahead and persevering no matter what.

We Can Do This Together

Broaching this topic of hope in the valleys of life is delicate work that is easily and, sadly, often too brusquely handled. It's tempting to stand on the other side of the valley and simply beckon the hurting to "just keep plowing forward." But, when someone jumps into the mess and sludges through the muck and mire with you, that makes all the difference. Or when someone admits to their own discouragement and struggle, you suddenly realize you aren't as alone as you often feel.

As I prepared the "Hope Rising" message I mentioned earlier, our family dog, Abby, passed away. Abby had originally belonged to my aunt. About a year after she died, my husband and I adopted her and brought her into our home. She was a part of our family almost from the beginning of our marriage. Her passing touched a part of me that I thought was long buried. My grief over losing my aunt all those years ago was stirred again.

The fifteen years we had with Abby were fifteen years we didn't get to have with my aunt, Lorie. Abby welcomed each of our three kids home from the hospital, and she lived in every one of our houses. Abby's habit of running around the house when she got excited spurred on our daughter's first laugh. And "Abby" was each of our kids' first words because we always said it when she was doing something naughty. Abby was there for all life had for us—the highs and the lows.

Lorie, however, barely met my husband—my boyfriend at the time. She was in remission when he first came to live in Oklahoma, and then, all of a sudden, she wasn't anymore. Before we knew it, we were camped at her bedside, watching her slowly slip away. She wasn't there for my wedding. She didn't get to celebrate with me at any of my baby showers. She didn't get to hold and smell and squish and kiss my babies. She never had the chance to pinch their bottoms like she did mine when I was little. She never heard me teach the Word of God or even knew it was a gift God had given me. And she won't get to read this book.

Even while reeling with these resurfaced feelings of loss, I could stand in front of our church and declare that our hope must rise. I wasn't proclaiming that as someone unfazed by the blows of this world or someone far removed from pain and sorrow. My heart wrenched as I shared about Abby and her connection to my aunt. I knew I couldn't authentically exhort them to hold onto hope even in the tough times if I was unwilling to admit I was wading through a valley I thought I had crossed long ago. I wasn't calling from some safe place above them. I was right there with them, whispering at their side, "We can do this together."

Is It Too Small a Thing?

Is it too small this thing we call hope? We know the end of the story, and it is even better than we can imagine. Is that not enough? Do we need all the details to move forward without fear? Is God's big plan not enough to fill us with hope for tomorrow and today? Does this hope not affect our day-to-day lives, touching every monumental and ordinary part of our days?

Is it too small a thing—this hope? No. No, it is not!

Our solid and secure hope, anchored in Christ, can infiltrate all the nooks and crannies of our lives if we let it. We are barraged by countless unknowns every single day. When we turn on the news, scroll through social media, and even talk with our neighbors and friends, we are bombarded with fear, division, nonsense, and even some real, scary stuff. It's everywhere. Fear is rising in our world. That fear isn't afraid to bust through closed doors, finding its way into the inner depths of our lives. But it is no match for solid, unshakable, formidable hope!

The darkness of the world cannot win against the light of the world: "The light shines in the darkness, and the darkness can never extinguish it" (John 1:5 NLT). The Light of the world is Jesus—God made flesh. Our hope.

This big hope provided for us through our big God's big plan is no small thing, and it does no small thing in us. This formidable hope frees us to live big now, even if it all feels so insignificant. It convinces us that our days are in His hands and that our lives are precious because of the price paid for them. Hope keeps us chugging forward in the good times and the difficult times, in the happy times and the crushing times, in the flourishing times and the hidden times. Hope breathes life into our very souls.

Hold fast your hope, friend.

Make This Prayer Yours

Lord, I know you are good and faithful. I know you are unfailing in your love for me, but sometimes I still feel hopeless and discouraged. I'm thankful you have given me emotions and the ability to feel, but help me not to let my feelings drive my hope and faith in you. Remind me in those dark times of your light that penetrates even into the darkest of depths. Lord, I ask that the hope of living forever with you would keep me strong when I am weak. Help me remember that hope isn't just for tomorrow, however. It is for today, too! You are with me right now! Always here. My hope is you. You are my light, my salvation, and my hope. Thank you. In the name of Jesus, amen.

Notes

1. *Merriam-Webster Dictionary*, s.v. "dystopia (n)," accessed November 10, 2022, https://www.merriam-webster.com/dictionary/dystopia.

2. Dallas Willard, *The Divine Conspiracy: Rediscovering Our Hidden Life in God* (London: William Collins, 2014), 19.

Rahab's Story

Found in Joshua 2 and 6

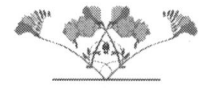

But I'm nobody. I'm just one person.

How could this one thing make any difference?

Does this even matter?

Do I even matter?

Doubts may have flooded in as the king of Jericho's men surged into Rahab's humble home. Should she give up the Israelite men who were hiding on her roof? What would happen to her and her family if they were found? Can she *really* do this? Is it really that important?

Relief must have washed over her as she ran to the roof to free the two men hiding there. She had convinced the king's men, now gone, that the Israelites had left toward the gates before the sun had set. She did it! Rahab saved the lives of the Israelite men, and in turn, they agreed to save her and her family's lives when they returned to overtake the city.

The Israelite men were under the orders of Joshua, the leader of God's people after the death of Moses. It was finally time for God's people to enter God's promised land after forty years in the desert, following their deliverance from Egypt and the miraculous splitting of the Red Sea. Jericho, where Rahab lived, was the beginning. These men were sent to spy on the land before the Israelite army came to conquer it.

Following their agreed-upon plan, Rahab tied a simple thread of scarlet in the window of her home, located along the city wall. Then, she waited. She had to trust the word of the two Israelite men—that they would spare her and her family's lives. I wonder, did those doubt-filled thoughts come knocking again?

But I'm nobody. I'm just one person.

How could this one thing make any difference?

Does this even matter?

Do I even matter?

Unsure and doubting what little she had done, wondering if it was enough to warrant her and her family's safety, Rahab had to trust and wait. That's all she could do. The scarlet thread was where it was supposed to be, and hopefully, it would be seen and honored.

When the Israelites began marching around Jericho, Rahab had to wonder whether they had forgotten about her. Every day, they marched, marched, and marched. Around and around. Trumpets were blown, but no sound, no shouts from the men. Maybe Rahab watched them from her window, the scarlet thread in her view, wondering where her salvation was.

On the seventh day, when the trumpets sounded, the men began to shout. This was different. The walls fell. The men charged forward, storming the city. Could she see them coming? What was going to happen to Rahab and her family?

Maybe it was a knock at the door. Or perhaps the men climbed up and in through the window. Or they might have burst right through the door, rushing to get to everyone waiting inside. In whatever way it happened, Rahab and her family were saved. The two spies from before found the little scarlet thread tied in the window of the humble home along the city wall. They ushered Rahab and all her family to safety. Rahab's actions mattered. That little thread mattered. She mattered.

But her story doesn't stop there...

Part 2

Is It Too Small a Thing...
What Is in Front of You?

In this second part of the book, we will ask our now favorite question in a more personal manner. The groundwork has been laid, and our perspective has been clarified. Now, let's build upon it.

In this section, we will:

- Wrestle with how we think about our regular, ordinary days and aspire to open our eyes to the beauty and goodness around us.
- Discover that everyday faithfulness matters now because what we do today affects who we will become tomorrow.
- Learn that the small things we do for others can make a difference—that these things are, in fact, ministry.

This portion of the book is all about learning to live with purpose and intention no matter the circumstances or situations in which we may find ourselves—and no matter what it may look like. Today matters. Whatever—or whoever—is in front of you right now is no small thing.

Chapter 5
Finding Beauty in the Ordinary

A curious thing happened when a warm, squirmy bundle of sweetness with ten fingers and ten toes was placed in my arms for the first time. My capacity for love expanded, swelling with every tiny exhale and every pitter-pat of her heart. Yet, at that moment, my world shrunk to the exact size of the seven-pound-thirteen-ounce baby girl nestled on my chest. In a single instant, my life soared to new heights while becoming more focused and smaller than ever.

Feeding, burping, changing, rocking, patting, shushing, crying, and sleeping (sometimes) comprised my life as a new mom. Overnight, these tasks became the new rhythm of life, the rhythm of motherhood. None of it was singular to me, of course. Mothers have been rocking these rhythms since the dawn of time.

That bundle of tiny fingers and toes quickly grew—just as we were warned she would. Not surprisingly, we added a couple more bundles into the mix over the next few years. The cadence of my days became so predictable that I wondered if I would ever know anything different. I felt lost in the beautiful yet hauntingly familiar refrain of motherhood.

There was a particular season in which I sobbed in the shower nearly every morning while whisper-praying for strength and joy. Out of conviction and often desperation, I would profess, "This is the day You have made, and I will rejoice and be glad in it. Thank you, Lord, for making me for *this* day." Some days I believed it; other days, I struggled. For a long period, the only thing getting me through each day was the promise of naptime and bedtime.

As a stay-at-home mom, my days blurred one into the other, but that phenomenon doesn't belong only to mothers. Whether you are a teacher, a bank teller, an engineer, a nurse, a college student, a retiree, or you name it, days have a way of suddenly becoming weeks, months, and even years. In one way or another, we are all familiar with the repetitiveness of life, the monotony of our days. And more often than not, it makes us feel so small, so insignificant.

Have you ever woken up reluctant to start the new day because you know it will feel so much like the day before?

Do you reach for a good book, wanting to get swept up in the story when real life has lost its appeal?

How about your relationship with Netflix or Hulu? Do you binge one show after the other because it's the only excitement you're likely to experience this week?

Or maybe you immerse yourself in work and unending checklists to help find meaning in your otherwise unchanging life.

Do you find your life too familiar, too predictable at times?

Comfort can be found in the familiar, but, in my case, the familiar felt restraining. Honestly, that revealed more about me than my circumstances. My situation didn't need to change; *I* needed to change. *I* was the problem. The issue was how I thought about my life and how I viewed what God had given me. It was an outward sign of the state of my heart—the innermost part of me—and it became apparent I needed a heart renovation.

To be clear, the heart change I required was not salvation. God had already done that work in me years before. Even though I was a "new creation," living the new kind of life promised to all believers, I still needed maintenance (2 Corinthians 5:17). The same can be said of all of us. We can be part of the family of God but forget exactly who we are in Him. We must remind ourselves what is true and vital in the Kingdom of God. That will be required of us every day of our lives.

Think on These Things

Near the end of his letter to the church in Philippi, the Apostle Paul offers some final pieces of instruction and wisdom. He emphasizes prayer, gratitude, and contentment—each vital for every healthy believer. He also instructs the Philippian church concerning their thought life. He writes: "...whatever is true, whatever is honorable, whatever is just, whatever is pure, whatever is lovely, whatever is commendable, if there is any excellence, if there is anything worthy of praise, think about these things" (Philippians 4:8 ESV). The placement of this particular instruction reveals the significance of maintaining one's thought life. It's sandwiched between the aforementioned prayer, gratitude, and contentment, leading to this conclusion: The direction of one's thoughts is no small thing.

Paul's call to be intentional with our habitual thoughts is not a one-time, last-minute tack-on to other, more significant teachings.

In fact, we are presented with the weightiness of how and what we think in Paul's letter to the Romans. He asserts that we are to be "transformed by the renewal of [our minds]" (Romans 12:1 ESV). That's probably the most familiar version. However, I want to offer this translation: "...let God transform you into a new person by changing the way you think" (NLT).

Changing how we think leads to a transformation—a renovation if you will.

Both of these verses from Paul live within a deeper and specific context. He speaks to legitimate issues while encouraging their thoughts toward the truth of who God is, what He has done, and the subsequent hope available to all believers. Since we spent the whole first part of this book addressing each of those remarkable truths, I'd like to tease out how tending to our thought life helps us in our everyday, ordinary lives thousands of years later. How should what we know and believe to be true affect our thoughts, and how does that begin to transform us?

Paul wrote his letter to the Philippians, which is full of encouragement, joy, and genuine affection, during a less than convenient time in his life and ministry. At the very least, he was under house arrest. Or worse, he was confined in prison, living in squalor with a severe lack of freedom. Either way, his circumstances were not in his control. Perhaps, every day looked and felt like a copy of the day before. Where he went and what he was allowed to do was limited. Maybe the familiarity of his days was heightened by actual restraints placed on his body. While his choices were physically limited, he still had the freedom to determine the condition of his mind and where he directed his thoughts.

In his book on Christian discipleship, Dallas Willard

maintains that "the mind...is the place of our widest and most basic freedom...Of all the things we do, we have more freedom with respect to *what we will think of*, where we will place our mind, than anything else."[1] I don't know about you, but I have yet to experience any restrictions enforced on my mind from an outside source. Our minds are free to roam and wander no matter the physical circumstances we find ourselves enduring—good or bad. A marker of spiritual growth, or that of a maturing disciple of Christ, is the willingness and ability to reign in one's innate wandering of the mind. Our ability to "think on these things," as Paul says, directly influences our outlook on life and the significance we ascribe to even the most mundane moments (Philippians 4:8 KJV).

That begs a few questions: What comes to mind when you think about your life? Where do your thoughts go? Do you try to wrangle your thoughts and guide them toward what is true, commendable, and lovely?

We all have good days and *less-than-good* days. Some mornings, we wake up refreshed and ready to tackle whatever the day holds. Other mornings, we sleep through our alarms and wake up to the sound of our 9-year-old son complaining about not having clean underwear for the day—something he could have told us the night before when we would have had time to do a load of laundry. All I'm saying is that some days it's easier to keep our minds on the "whatever is true...whatever is lovely" way of thinking. And other days, we desperately want to wallow in the dangerously enticing trap of *nothing is lovely*. Growth is recognizing the lure of lazy, negative thinking and choosing to "think on these things" instead.

Let's do some thought replacement practice.

Stuck in this thought trap?	Think THIS instead!
I woke up late! Now my day is going to be absolute chaos. This is going to be the worst day!	Thank you, God, I woke up today! I have breath in my lungs and blood pumping through my body. I may be behind already, but I know I can still walk in your peace today.
Money is tight this month. Who am I kidding? It's tight every month. It's peanut butter and jelly sandwiches again for dinner, and my kids are wearing their cousins' hand-me-downs. We're never going to get anywhere in life at this rate.	I'm so thankful my kids are healthy, and they don't mind eating peanut butter and jelly sandwiches. I'm so amazed at how excited they are when they get new clothes from their cousins. Times are tough for us right now, but I know God is taking care of us.
I yelled at my kids *again* tonight. I'm a horrible mom. My kids would be so much better off with someone else. I can't seem to do anything right in life, especially for my kids.	My children are a blessing, and they continue to love me even when I mess up. How amazing are they! I know God is with me as I try to love them and guide them. I'm thankful I'm not on my own.

I feel worthless. Every day is the same. Does anyone even notice me at all? Does anything I do actually matter?	God sees me and loves me. That can be enough for me today. I wonder if there is anyone I can encourage today. Maybe it's my turn to notice someone else.

Somewhere in the Middle

Life is often compared to mountains and valleys—in the Bible, songs, and books. Those high and low moments become the fence posts, the pivotal experiences, that structure our lives. But, just like a fence is incomplete without the pickets filling in the space between each post, our lives are considerably more than just highs and lows. Our days consist of far more regular, simple, and easily overlooked moments. When we live for the mountain-top experiences, merely enjoying the pinnacle of the climb, or live absorbed and overwhelmed by the valleys, we miss out on all the beauty and goodness of life found while we are somewhere in the middle.

Chances are that you are somewhere in the middle right now. Life is good…or at least it's moving along. Sure, situations could be better, but they could also be worse. The middle is safe. It could even be seen as a gift. It's in these ordinary, regular days that you have the opportunity, if you so choose it, to notice the little things. If you train yourself to see the beauty of your days, wherever you are or whatever you are doing, your days will become more beautiful.

Finding the lovely in your regular, daily life is a worthy aspiration, but it requires effort. My goal is to encourage, yes, but also to equip you with the desire and discipline to become someone whose second nature is to see, cherish, and celebrate beauty in the ordinary. How can you train yourself to "stop and smell the roses," as they say? What would it look like in your daily life to begin appreciating the beauty and goodness (and significance, because that often follows) right where you are?

- Journal it. Take a few minutes each evening to record something simple about your day.
- Start a text group with your friends or family. When you notice something lovely during your day, share it with the group.
- Take a picture—you could just keep it in an album on your phone or post it on social media. Who cares what other people think?
- Or keep it simple and verbally acknowledge the beauty when you see it, taking it a bit further than merely thinking about it.

Maybe you want to protest this idea of beauty being all around you. You can acknowledge the splendor of a sunset or an unexpected rainbow. You can even admit to enjoying a field of wildflowers or the trees at the peak of autumn. But, beauty in your regular, day-to-day life when one day melds into the other and you sincerely lose track of what day it is?

Yes! Loveliness lurks around every corner; it lingers long enough for us to notice if we will have eyes and hearts open to seeing it. In the beginning, it'll surprise us, showing up somewhere least expected. Eventually, however, we'll be more surprised when we don't see it—when beauty evades even the most ordinary days.

I firmly believe that you can find beauty and goodness even in the messiest of messes and most mundane moments. Sometimes you just have to change your perspective or look a little closer.

FINDING BEAUTY IN THE ORDINARY

Are your kids' rooms a disaster, with toys strewn everywhere? Zoom in a little and take notice of your son's smile as he puts all those Lego pieces together, creating his own little wonder.

Are you staring at dishes overflowing in the sink or piles of laundry that more resemble mountains than clothes? Take a closer look and see the full bellies and warm bodies contributing to that mess.

Do you spend untold hours in your car, driving from here to there and back again? You have the opportunity to watch the changing of the seasons happen right before your eyes. Yesterday the trees were some sort of fading green and tired from the scorching sun of summertime, but today, all of a sudden, the colors of fall have erupted all over those worn-out trees!

The twinkling stars light up the night sky as you take your dog out one final time for the night. Your coworkers laughing and genuinely enjoying each other's company amidst a frantic season of software updates and personnel shifts. The lines on your neighbor's freshly mowed lawn (because you haven't had time to take care of yours yet.) The warm mug of coffee in your hands on a crisp morning or a steaming cup of tea in the evening after the kids have finally gone to bed. The way the evening sun shines *just right* through your front windows, casting that perfect glow on your family as they settle in to watch a show.

I'm telling you—beauty is all around. Your mission, should you accept it, is to look, *honestly look*, for it.

Please understand that I'm not just encouraging you to look differently at your life to find it more pleasing or enjoyable. Remember what Paul told us—changing the way we *think* leads to transformation. I'm inviting you to open your eyes to the goodness of the life in front of you right now because what you notice and pay attention to has a way of infiltrating your thoughts. It becomes what you think about. Training yourself to see the good, lovely, and beautiful is one way to change the way you think, leading to transformation from the inside out.

Everyday Beauty, Everyday Praise

If we keep the proper perspective in life, remembering our big God, His big plan, and the big hope He offers for today and tomorrow, something extraordinary happens right in the middle of our ordinary. Those little pockets of loveliness? They not only begin filling our thoughts, but they begin forming our praise. The everyday beauty around us is turned into everyday praise to God. Yes, we become more grateful for the little things in life. More than that, though, we begin to recognize the good and beautiful everyday realities as glimpses into our God's very goodness and beauty. We learn to ask, just as Timothy Keller quotes C.S. Lewis asking, "What *kind* of God would create this, give me this?"[2] How good and beautiful and lovely *He* must be!

This idea of everyday beauty became a life-changing theme in my early years of motherhood when I was elbow deep in diapers and onesies. By God's grace, I recognized that the direction my thoughts were taking me was nowhere healthy or good for my family or me.

God woke me up and opened my eyes to the beauty within even the smallest of moments. The way my youngest always slept with his little bum in the air. How my daughter loved to twirl and skip. My middle child's ability to know *exactly* what he liked and didn't like. The way all three of them played and giggled.

We began taking walks around our tiny neighborhood, often

described as city in the front and country in the back. As the seasons changed, we took notice of the little buds forming on the trees and bushes, checking them every day in anticipation of them blooming. And when they finally did, we reveled in the sheer loveliness of God's creation. Slowly, I began loving and enjoying and delighting in my life again.

Nothing about my situation changed. I was still a stay-at-home mom with a husband who worked well over forty hours during the week and served at church with most of his free time (something about which we have since had many conversations). My youngest was still in the middle of sleep training and waking up all hours of the night. The other two still woke up earlier than I would prefer in the mornings. All of it was the same. *I* had changed—or had begun to change. During those years, God began molding, pruning, and nudging—slowly and tenderly doing His deepest work in me. (We'll talk more about this in the following chapters.)

Back in the heyday of Mommy blogs and the early years of Instagram, I began recording my beauty-in-the-ordinary findings, hoping to encourage other moms along the way. That initial blog didn't last long. Instagram, however, became my favorite mode of preserving the everyday moments I never wanted to forget, and, of course, I even created a hashtag to keep it all together.

Occasionally, I look up #MyEverydayisBeautiful, and I'm so thankful I captured those moments. I notice how happy my kids were and how much they enjoyed life—even when every day felt the same as the day before. As I scroll through image after image, I remember the tears, the laughter, the delight, and even the struggles of those cherished years. It's almost enough to make me want to travel back to that time. Almost.

I'm convinced the softening of my heart happened as I began

cherishing the small moments of my every day and noticing the good, beautiful, and lovely. My thoughts changed course. No longer was I dreading the day as I woke every morning. I still prayed in the shower, thanking God for the day and asking for strength and patience, but rarely out of desperation. My days were never perfect, and I was not immune to that *nothing-is-lovely* trap. Mostly, I was able to recognize it quicker and free myself more easily from its vice grip.

Even now, as I sit here typing these words, drinking tea from my favorite mug that happens to say "love the little things" on it, I'm realizing how instrumental those tender years were to my overall personal growth—spiritual, mental, and physical. While I no longer share photos tagged with that hashtag (maybe I should start again), I still intentionally look for the lovely and beautiful in my day. Some days it is easily found in the physical beauty around me, and other days I have to dig a little deeper, look a little closer to find it. This is a discipline I'm committed to practicing all the days of my life because I *know* it is directly linked to my willingness and ability to "think on these things."

Changing how we think about our everyday lives doesn't make us any more important or influential in this world. It won't change our status or stature. It won't automatically win us more followers or friends. That's okay because it's not about what happens on the outside. It's about the significant work happening on the inside.

Is It Too Small a Thing?

Friend, is it too small a thing to begin changing the way we think about our regular, everyday lives? Is noticing and delighting in the beauty, goodness, and loveliness of today not enough to begin altering how we view our lives as a whole? Or, is our ordinary day-to-day utterly devoid of anything good or worthy of being enjoyed or praised?

No!

Even though I don't know what your life looks like or the pain and struggle you may be experiencing (or have experienced), I do know a few things about you. I know you were intricately formed and knitted together by the mighty, loving hands of God (Psalm 139:13). I know God loves you more than you can comprehend, and nothing—not a bad day, a good day, a stumble along the way, or even your doubt about His goodness—can separate you from His love (Romans 8:35-39). I know it gave God immense pleasure to bring you into His family, to call you one of His own through Jesus Christ. From the beginning, it was His plan to open His arms and heart to you (Ephesians 1:5-6).

Knowing *that* is who God is, how could we ever question the beauty and goodness of our days? Even on our worst days, He is the loveliness we seek. He is what we should think about in order to transform our lives truly. The small delights of our ordinary days are tiny glimmers of the utter splendor and glory of our God.

Is it too small a thing to begin noticing the beauty of our ordinary days? No, because it is how we learn to open ourselves—our eyes and hearts—to God, who is the source of everything good, lovely, and beautiful. Our ordinary days are the training ground for truly appreciating and reverencing the extraordinariness of our God.

Make This Prayer Yours

Lord, I want to see the beauty of my ordinary days, my boring days, my busy days, and even my broken days. I'm sorry for all the times I have complained about what I have in front of me—my job, my family, my friends (or lack thereof), and everything else. Help me change the way I think about today and tomorrow as I try to find the lovely within my days. Help me notice the good. Help me find *you* today. If there are wrong thoughts I need to remove from my habitual thinking, I'm thankful you will help me. But more than that, help me replace them with what is lovely and true and good. Today is a gift; help me remember that. In the name of Jesus, amen.

Notes

1. Dallas Willard, *The Divine Conspiracy: Rediscovering Our Hidden Life in God* (London: William Collins, 2014), 355.

2. Timothy Keller, *Prayer: Experiencing Awe and Intimacy with God* (New York: Penguin Books, 2016), 197.

Chapter 6
Everyday Faithfulness Matters

My grandmother passed away last year. She lived a long, fulfilling life—though not without heartache and loss. She loved her family and friends, and most importantly, she loved Jesus.

The last time I was with her, just days before she passed, she had such an urgency to pray for my husband and me. Multiple times during our short 30-minute visit, her frail, bony hands reached for ours as she prayed. "Oh, Father," she began, "I pray for my friends today. Fill them with your joy and peace. Help them to know Your love for them." She had dementia and could not even remember who we were at this point, but it did not stop her from proclaiming God's love over us.

We chatted with her as best we could. She had only a few things to say, most of which she repeated several times. She confided in us, as though it were a secret, that she preferred to fill her time simply talking to Jesus. As we prepared to leave, knowing it would likely be the last time we would see her this side of eternity, I grabbed her tiny hands and began praying for her. I prayed her prayer, asking God to fill her with joy and peace and to consume her with His love. We walked away comforted, knowing she would soon be with Jesus and reunited with many of our loved ones.

Being faced with mortality has a way of putting life in perspective. There is an end. That's the one guarantee about life; it will end at some point and in some way. As much as we would prefer it, we don't usually have a say about when the end will come. But *who* we are when it arrives is something within our control. The kind of person we have become—whether or not we have used all that life has thrown at us to become more like Christ—is entirely up to us.

What kind of woman do I want to be when I'm 87 years old?

That question rattled around inside every part of my being for days after that final visit with my grandmother. It finally settled deep within me, anchoring itself with another pivotal question.

What am I doing today *that will help me become that kind of woman?*

The years aren't slowing down. A new day dawns every twenty-four hours without fail. That someday far off in the distance is coming, and who we are when it gets here is determined by what we do today, tomorrow, and the next day.

Everyday faithfulness matters.

What kind of person do *you* want to be when you are 87 years old? What are you doing *today* that will help you become that kind of person? The ordinariness of today and what you do with it—even if it feels small and insignificant—shapes your tomorrow.

EVERYDAY FAITHFULNESS MATTERS

Thirty Years of Ordinariness

In her exploration of the ordinary, Tish Harrison Warren observes this about Jesus: "The one who is worthy of worship, glory, and fanfare spent decades in obscurity and ordinariness. As if the incarnation itself is not mind-bending enough, the incarnate God spent His days quietly, a man who went to work, got sleepy, and lived a pedestrian life among average people."[1]

We know very little about the three decades of Jesus's life that led up to His three years of public ministry. I'm sure those years were formative for Jesus; they certainly are for us. Even though Jesus was fully God walking on this earth, He was also fully man. In Hebrews, it says He experienced everything we experience—all the trials and temptations—because of His humanity (Hebrews 4:15). That's what makes Him the perfect mediator and sacrifice for our sins—the One we (all of humanity) desperately needed.

I don't think it's too much to assume that Jesus knew ordinary. He knew living small and quiet. He woke up every morning with the same choice we have: to be open to what the day holds and live it according to the will of God. Jesus learned, played, served, worked, worshiped, ate, drank, and slept. He knew doing the right thing even if it was hard. He knew showing up even when He was tired. He knew using what He had right in front of Him for the glory of God and the good of others. He knew everyday faithfulness, and He lived it perfectly.

Even though He lived a "pedestrian life," Jesus was able to live with the end in mind. He knew where the everyday moments were leading Him. That's the key to living well and faithfully in the ordinariness and, sometimes, drudgery of life.

Jesus is our model of faithfulness.

It would be naive to assume that Jesus's most extraordinary act of faithfulness was unrelated to His lifetime of entirely ordinary acts of faithfulness. His sacrifice on the cross—giving His life for us—was tethered to His daily sacrifices of self offered among people who refused to acknowledge the very "image of the invisible God" walking in their midst (Colossians 1:15 ESV). And, yet, He was not only able but *willing* to surrender His life and eternal communion with the Father for those very people.

As He endured the loss of all He had ever known, He looked forward with joy toward what He would gain, which is why we are encouraged to look to Him as we run our race here on earth (Hebrews 12:2). He knew the present hardship He was experiencing, even His own death, was not the end of the story. He fixed His eyes on the prize ahead, full of faith and expectancy of the joy found there. The joy of reunion with the Father and His eternal union with His body, the Church—those who faithfully believe and live according to His commands.

A few chapters back, we discovered that the prize awaiting us at the end is God Himself. He will be with us, and we will be with Him (Revelation 21:3)! When we follow Jesus's example and fix our gaze on the end goal—living forever *with* Him—then every moment, every step, every choice gains new and deeper meaning. Today is what leads to tomorrow, which eventually leads to eternity. Today—and all the small things it holds—is significant no matter how ordinary and plain it is.

If thirty years of ordinariness was good for Jesus, then who are we to begrudge 60, 70, or even 80 years of it? If we can't find meaning and significance in the simplicity and repetitiveness of life, then maybe we're not fully living as God intended. And if our daily lives hold no plan to ensure we remain along the path of faithfulness, how would we expect to be found faithful at the end?

The Path of Faithfulness

Remember our discussion about mountains and valleys in the previous chapter? Life is often compared to those highs and lows. Life is also frequently referred to as a path, especially in the Bible. It's a theme with roots planted back in the beginning with Adam and Eve. The course set before them was one of faithfulness, devoted love and loyalty, and obedience to God. Yet, as we've already addressed, they chose a different way.

Mankind has struggled with opposing paths since the garden. It's *still* our struggle. Throughout Scripture, we read about God's people following His path, stumbling from His path, refusing His path, and sometimes even finding His path again. Prophets, psalmists, and apostles, inspired by the Holy Spirit, include path imagery in their Biblical writings. Psalm 1, for example, contains admonition against the path of the wicked and encouragement toward the way of the righteous: "For the Lord watches over the path of the godly, but the path of the wicked leads to destruction" (v. 6 NLT).

When we strip everything else away, when we get to the very core of our purpose here on earth, we find only one way paved for us. There is only one path we are meant to follow. Sadly, that has never kept people, us included, from forging their own paths through the rugged terrain of life, and where those many paths lead is destruction. Jesus Himself depicts the single, faithful path as one with a "narrow gate," but "the gate is wide and the way is easy that leads to destruction and those who enter by it are many" (Matthew 7:13 ESV).

To better shine light on the path of faithfulness, we're going to take a closer look at the *unfaithfulness* of God's people during the time of the prophet Jeremiah. Numerous prophets over hundreds of years warned their people about the coming judgment due to their wandering and utter unfaithfulness. Jeremiah was God's final attempt to grab the hearts of His people, but, spoiler alert, their hearts were too hardened.

In Jeremiah 6:16, God said, "Stand by the roads, and look, and ask for the ancient paths, where the good way is; and walk in it, and find rest for your souls. But they said, 'We will not walk in it'" (ESV). This ancient path, the "good way," was the original course they were meant to follow. The way that would lead them to God, to the *only* God. He was calling them back to the path of faithfulness, but they refused to follow it. More than that, though, they rejected Him.

Here's what we must understand: The path of faithfulness does not lead us *somewhere*; it leads us to *someone*. The way God has set before us is not the way of religion or simply a better life. It is the very highway to Him.

The Israelites missed this point—or maybe they didn't care. As we attempt to understand faithfulness better, even the ordinary, everyday kind, let's learn from what the Israelites did not do.

1. **Know God**

    First of all, the path of faithfulness requires that we know God. Reading through Jeremiah, we could pull from multiple examples where God Himself indicts His people for their lack of knowing Him. He says, "They only go from bad to worse. They do not know me" (Jeremiah 9:3 NLT). Later in that chapter, God declares His people should refrain from boasting about their wisdom, strength, or riches. He says, "Let him who boasts boast in this, that he understands and knows me" (v. 24 ESV). Even Paul, centuries later, points back to these words from God, revealing that he considers "everything else is worthless when compared with the infinite value of knowing Christ Jesus" (Philippians 3:8 NLT).

Knowing God is essential along the path of faithfulness. Of course, it is! Yet, God's people in the Old Testament did not know Him. Over the generations, they had forgotten who He was and what He had done for them.

2. **Love God**
The path of faithfulness also requires that we love God. In fact, our knowing God leads to loving Him. The more we know Him—not just *about* Him, mind you—the more we will love Him.
This, too, the Israelites did not do. When God asks His people, "When will you stop running? When will you stop panting after other gods?" He says their response is as if they are saying, "'Save your breath. I'm in love with these foreign gods, and I can't stop loving them now'" (2:25 NLT). And even Jeremiah himself says of the people, "Your name is on their lips, but You are far from their hearts" (12:2 NLT). The people of Israel had no love for God.

3. **Live For God**
Lastly, the path of faithfulness requires that we live for God. But, once again, this flows from knowing and loving Him. The more we know Him, the more we love Him, and we will desire to live for Him, to please Him. This last one is unavoidable, lest we become hypocrites— much like the Pharisees of Jesus's day.

The Israelites refused to live to please God. That way

of life had long passed their hearts and minds. Remember their response to God's ancient path: "We will not walk in it" (Jeremiah 6:16 ESV). Their refusal led to their loss of land, home, and way of life. Eventually, most of them were taken captive and brought to live in Babylon—in exile.

But God, being true to form, already had a plan. Even while they were living in a foreign land, desperate to return home, God offered, once again, a way to live that would please Him. In Jeremiah 29, through a letter written by the prophet, God instructs His people to

> Build homes, and plan to stay. Plant gardens, and eat the food they produce. Marry and have children. Then find spouses for them so that you may have many grandchildren. Multiply! Do not dwindle away! And work for the peace and prosperity of the city where I sent you into exile. Pray to the
> LORD for it, for its welfare will determine your welfare (vs. 5-7 NLT).

"Live," God told them. "But, now, try *living for me*. Try it my way—the good way." Just after this instruction, God informed them they will be living in exile for seventy years! He wanted them to dig deep roots, to be in it for the long haul.

The path of faithfulness, the highway of life that God desires each of us to walk, consists of daily, consistent steps in the shape of knowing Him, loving Him, and living for Him. It sounds simple because He meant it to be simple. He wants to meet us at the end of the path; He wants us to succeed!

EVERYDAY FAITHFULNESS MATTERS

You already know I have struggled with failure in my life. I even used to fight fears of failure when it came to my relationship with God. *What if I don't make it to the end faithfully with God? What if I fail at the biggest, most important thing in life?*

As I have progressed along this path of faithfulness—knowing, loving, and living for God—I have dropped my fear of failure! I no longer fear that I won't make it to the end because the end isn't necessarily my goal anymore. *He* is my goal. As I move forward, step by step, I keep my eyes on Him. I keep my gaze and my hope on Him! And that changes everything.

How do we make it to the end faithfully? By taking daily steps toward our God. Keeping our gaze on Him and remembering this is as personal for Him as it is for us.

Everyday faithfulness—putting one foot in front of the other—is the only way to complete the path. It's small and consistent movement toward Him.

As we continue putting in the effort to know, love, and live for Him, I believe our lives will begin to fulfill the Romans 12:1 way of living: "Present your bodies as a living sacrifice, holy and acceptable to God, which is your spiritual worship" (ESV). To drive it all the way home, here it is in the MESSAGE paraphrase: "Take your everyday, ordinary life—your sleeping, eating, going to work, and walking-around life—and place it before God as an offering."

Our entire lives—the whole story from beginning to messy middle to end—is our offering, our gift to God. It's how we say "thank you" for who He is, what He has done, and the hope He has given us. Everyday faithfulness matters.

Let's Get Practical

I know I said this whole *path of faithfulness* thing is simple, and I stand by it. It is simple in theory but not always in practice. The path of faithfulness is the way of discipleship. And just as that word implies, it requires discipline, especially of the everyday variety.

Let's talk about some specific practices, or disciplines, we will need to pick up as we endeavor to follow the path of faithfulness. For obvious reasons, this will not be an exhaustive list. Time and space will only allow for addressing a few disciplines. But we all have to start somewhere, right?

As we briefly discuss the following practices, it is important for you to know that it takes time to develop new habits in our lives. That's what these are—spiritual habits. Remember: Small doesn't mean insignificant. Starting small, with just a little time, is *not* insignificant. A little bit can go a long way when we keep at it. Starting small is better than not starting at all.

How can we better KNOW GOD?

- **Bible Study** — Our Bibles are the primary way for us to better know God. Full stop. And I'm not merely talking about gaining more head knowledge about Him. He has chosen to reveal His character, desires, plan, and love through the very words we so often take for granted.

    To better know God as we read our Bibles, we have to approach our Bibles with Him in view. It's easy to open our Bibles and search for a verse or a passage that encourages us or speaks to our current situation. That's not necessarily wrong, but it short-changes us on all the Word of God holds for us. Scripture speaks of God and who He is more than about our situations. When we are convinced of and in awe of who He is, our life takes the proper position under Him. This is also why we began this book heavily emphasizing our big God!

Regarding Bible study, I ascribe to the quality-over-quantity mindset, meaning the truth you walk away with is more important than how much you actually read. This is especially true when we are in the early stages of cultivating this habit. However, that does not mean quantity is worthless or that we should not train ourselves to read more.

I also adhere to the idea that we need both depth *and* breadth.[2] It's vital to know the big story of the Bible—to read all of it—while also taking time to dig deeper into smaller sections and books. Both are necessary, but both don't have to be done at the same time. For example, over the past few years, I have alternated between reading the Bible in a year and slowly digging into single books. One year, I read for breadth. The following year, I choose a few books or particular passages to read and study for depth.

- **Prayer** — Another primary way we can better know God is through prayer. I mentioned Bible study first because I believe a right and Biblical approach to prayer only comes from a solid foundation in the Word. Timothy Keller says prayer, in the fullest sense, is "continuing a conversation that God has started through His Word and His grace which eventually becomes a full encounter with Him."[3]

Often, we have an overly religious or forced view of

prayer. It has to look like *this*, sound *that way*, or only include *these* words—all of which often lead to severe insecurity regarding prayer. As a pastor's wife and one who frequently prays publicly, with a microphone or simply an engaged diaphragm, I hear from women who shudder at the idea of praying in front of someone else. But we forget—or maybe never understood—that prayer is simply communicating with our Heavenly Father. It is spending time with Him, intentionally in His presence. There isn't an exact formula—not in the sense that we often want.[4] I even view my time in the Word and worship as prayer because it's all communication to and with my God.

Practically, if you are trying to cultivate a habit of daily prayer, try connecting it with something you already do consistently. Pray while you are in the shower. (This is one of my biggest "mom hacks!") Pray on your way to work or with your children on the way to school. Pray as you clean the kitchen and do the dishes. Pray when you walk your dog around the block. I'm not a betting woman, but I am willing to bet there are some routines already in your life that you could easily connect with your time in prayer. And once again, starting small is better than not starting at all!

How exactly do we LOVE GOD?

- **Obedience** — I'll keep this one short because there's a whole chapter coming up on this. It is essential to include here because obedience is the Biblical way we show and express our love for God. Let's go straight to what Jesus said in John 14:15: "If you love me, you will keep my commandments" (ESV). He repeats something to the same effect three more times within that chapter. And He even declares that His obedience to the Father—going to the cross—will reveal to the world His love for the Father (v. 31).

Love is tied to obedience, whether we like it or not. God directs us on how to live, lays out parameters, and asks us to obey Him. If we love Him, our obedience is the proof. That's a risky thing to say today, but I stand by it.

Obedience is a spiritual discipline you can cultivate in your life. Like with the other practices, it becomes easier the more you do it. Starting small is just as effective here. What's one thing you know the Word of God says you should do? Start with that. As you begin stretching your obedience muscle, you'll notice more and more directives in the Word and from the Spirit. Your "yes" will come more easily as you keep at it.

How are we supposed to LIVE FOR GOD?

The above disciplines are ways we begin living for God. Let's add to the list some other ways:

- Loving our neighbors well.

- Putting other people's needs above our wants.

- Living in community with other believers—church, small groups, home church, some form of intentional fellowship with people who also follow Jesus.

- Giving our resources toward His Kingdom—money, time, talents, and abilities.

- Loving our family—even the hard-to-love ones.

- Telling other people about the good news of Jesus Christ, which often looks like telling them how He has changed your life.

All of these are choices we make. We choose whether or not we will live in a way that pleases God, that becomes a gift to Him. Let's be encouraged that God does not expect us to be perfect, nor does He think we can do this all on our own.

Living this way is found along that ancient path. It's the journey of our life—one that will require our entire lifetime. But it all starts as simply as putting one foot in front of the other, deciding to start small in just one area of life today.

Knowing, loving, and living for God is the way of everyday faithfulness, the path that eventually ends when we are face-to-face with Him. Every day brings us closer to our prize. If we want to be found faithful at 87 years old, then it starts today. Right where we are, exactly as we are.

Starting Small

I know the exact point in time when I realized something entirely true yet awful about myself. I had become a hypocrite—someone who says one thing and does another. Or, as is often the case in the church world, someone who lets people assume the best while knowing what was going on behind the scenes. That's a harsh thing to say, and it's no easier to admit.

I've already told you how I grew up. You know that I attended a ministry internship, learned much about God that changed my life, and even went to Bible College afterward. However, after those intense years with God, my relationship with Him became stagnant. Yes, even while He was teaching me how to appreciate and enjoy the little things in life, I kept Him at arm's length while pretending (often unintentionally) to the outside world that I was as close as ever to Him.

The most obvious indicator of my hypocritical—or at the very least insincere—status was the thick, undisturbed layer of dust on my Bible. I couldn't even justify the dust by claiming to have been reading the Bible on my phone; the apps may have existed, but I didn't know about them yet. (These were early "smartphone" years.) Reading my Bible wasn't necessarily something I was choosing *not to do*, but it was something I was not choosing *to do*.

I've written openly about this time in my life on my blog and Instagram over the years.[5] The point I want to make here is that I chose to make a change, and I'm convinced God helped me. During the most inconvenient season of my life, I began reading my Bible again. I was still in the throes of raising my tiny tots. I didn't wait for perfect timing—is there even such a thing? I started small, finding pockets of time whenever I could.

As I stuck with it and continued reading, my desire for the Word grew. The more I read, the more I wanted to read—and dig deeper. I rearranged my schedule, making more time for the Word of God. What started as a small and slow adjustment to my everyday life ended up revolutionizing my entire life.

Eventually, I wasn't just reading the Bible. I found myself talking about it, thinking about it, writing about it, and living it out—letting it transform me from the inside out. IT CHANGED MY LIFE. The Word became my very source of hope, joy, and peace because I began to know my Lord and King through it intimately. *He* changed my life.

In fact, this book you are holding is a direct result of a daily decision to be faithful in reading my Bible. There were plenty of days in which I walked away from my time in the Word unaffected, unchanged, and not encouraged. There were days I completely skipped it, but I was determined to keep showing up—even if it was a week or two later. I kept showing up.

Can you see yourself somewhere in my story? Maybe not in connection with reading the Bible. Maybe the spiritual habit you are struggling with is one of the others I mentioned above. Friend, let me encourage you. Good things come with time. Please don't look for immediate results. Slow growth *is* growth; more often than not, it is the most sustainable kind of growth. The key here is sustainability. The path of faithfulness—living a life of everyday faithfulness—is a long road. Remember, God is playing the long game and looking for long-term growth that lasts the test of time.

Is It Too Small a Thing?

Is taking one step forward every day too small a thing? Is everyday, ordinary faithfulness not enough in the Kingdom of God? Is God only interested in the impressive, giant steps of faith that result in immediate growth and change? Is it too small a thing to live your daily life as faithfully as you can?

No!

Our lives are today. We can't get to tomorrow without today—funny how that works. If we can't learn to be faithful today, even just a tiny bit, the faithfulness we desire won't magically show up tomorrow. We will not, *cannot* drift toward faithfulness. It's not the current in which we swim in this broken and hurting world.

To get to the heart of this, I'll ask one more question:

EVERYDAY FAITHFULNESS MATTERS

Considering who God is and what He has done for you, is it not worth your effort and desire to live every day faithfully?

Your life is your response to Him. Wherever you go, whatever you do, every step, every decision, every word, and every action is your offering to God. When you think about it that way, every small thing is significant. Every moment matters. We all have to begin somewhere and often with whatever is in front of us. It's not about the size or outcome; it's all about your heart for Him.

Make This Prayer Yours

Lord, I want to live every day faithfully for you. I want my life to be a pleasing offering to you. Would you reveal areas in my life that are not pleasing to you? Will you show me ways I can begin to increase my faithfulness? I desire to know, love, and live for you, and I know that will require humble and intentional effort from me. When I stumble or get weary, I believe you will continue to be by my side, helping and guiding me. Even though it is up to me to remain on the path of faithfulness, I know I'm not alone. Thank you for being with me. Thank you for your faithfulness toward me. I don't deserve it, but I am thankful for it. In the name of Jesus, amen.

Notes

1. Tish Harrison Warren, *Liturgy of the Ordinary: Sacred Practices in Everyday Life* (Downers Grove, Illinois: IVP Books, 2016), chap. 1, Scribd.

2. Thank you to Jen Wilkin for this terminology.

3. Timothy Keller, *Prayer: Experiencing Awe and Intimacy with God* (New York: Penguin Books, 2016), 48.

4. Jesus does give His disciples directions on how to pray. Read Matthew 6:1-15. Rather than being rote words to recite, Jesus communicates the heart behind prayer. Timothy Keller's book on prayer, cited above, is also a great resource.

5. You can read more at RootedandStrong.com/blog or on Instagram (find me: @rooted.and.strong or @ashleylainekelly).

Chapter 7
The Ministry of Small Things

"Just try them," my husband practically begged one afternoon, a half-eaten taco in one hand and a jar of pickled red onions in the other.

Taco ingredients, left over from a small group dinner we had the night before, were strewn across the counter. It was lunchtime, and a leftover taco was sure to hit the spot. As I layered all my favorite toppings in a tortilla, my husband wouldn't give up on me trying the pickled red onions—even though he *knew* I despised raw onions.

I'm not sure what made me give in that day. Was it his incessant nagging? Was I too tired from the night before, causing a lapse in my better judgment? Or was I genuinely curious if those highly praised onions would take my taco to a new level?

Whatever caused me to stick my fork into the jar, wrangle a few onions on board, and then drape them on top of my otherwise perfect taco, I am now and forevermore grateful it did! I had no idea what my tastebuds were missing without those deliciously sweet and tangy pickled onions nestled among my other favorite flavors.

If you had told me the day before, when everyone else was gobbling up tacos laden with said onions, that I would one day be just like them, I would have laughed and refused to believe it. Not me! Not the girl who stubbornly picked every onion, chive, and anything else remotely onion-like out of every salad, casserole, pasta dish, fried rice, and stir fry. No way!

I have since made multiple jars of that sweet and tangy goodness. When we eat tacos at home, a weekly occurrence in our family, I am embarrassingly disappointed if I find the jar empty or missing in the fridge. (This reminds me that I need to buy another red onion!) A taco is no longer a taco without pickled red onions.

Is it too dramatic to say that a jar of homemade pickled red onions changed my life?

It seems like such a small thing—one extra topping on a simple taco. Inconsequential in the grand scheme of things. But if it brings a smile to my face and makes my stomach growl even now as I write this, then maybe it's not as little and silly as it seems.

Maybe something as small and seemingly insignificant as red onions soaked in vinegar, sugar, and salt does have the potential to make such a significant impact. Maybe little things matter more than we know. Maybe there is life-changing power in the small, overlooked, momentary stuff of life.

The Ministry Right in Front of You

I've become rather fond of thinking of this particular idea as "the ministry of small things." How often do we consider the possibility of regular, everyday, or even fleeting moments holding within them the ability to dramatically affect our lives and the lives of those around us? Of course, without much convincing, we affirm the impact that momentous occasions or events have on our lives. But those small, inconsequential, ordinary moments, could they really matter just as much or maybe even more?

What about the routine, commonplace, or simple things we do on a regular day? Could they have a lasting impact? A kind smile or wave to a stranger. A sincere compliment to a friend that would have been just as easy to keep to yourself. Leaving a quarter in your returned Aldi cart. (Have you ever been the recipient of that *small* kindness? It's just a quarter, but it brightens your whole day!) Saying "yes" to making a meal for a family who just brought home a new baby. Actually praying for someone when they ask for prayer. Sending a quick text to a friend just to let them know you have been thinking about them. Washing that never-ending sink full of dirty dishes without complaining—yes, even that!

All of these little efforts or small moments may not look or feel like much, but I hope by now I don't have to convince you that small doesn't mean insignificant. That the little things we do actually matter. These little things can brighten someone's day, make someone smile, and even shine a little hope into someone's gloom.

These "small things" are ministry, and maybe it's time we start recognizing them as such.

Ministry is not reserved for some religious elite. It is not only for those who are educationally qualified. Ministry is not merely about pulpits and sermons and perfectly exegeted Bible passages. Nope! Ministry is for all of God's people. It is found in every nook and cranny of life—of *your* life. Ministry is for everyday people living in the mundane predictability of everyday life.

In an article on Christianity.com, ministry is defined as "what we do for God's glory based on where He has placed us, how He has gifted us, and what He has called us to do according to His infinite wisdom and for the proclamation of the gospel."[1] According to this definition, ministry couldn't possibly be reserved for a select few. Scripture instructs all followers of Jesus—that includes us—to "do all to the glory of God" (1 Corinthians 10:31 ESV; also see Matthew 5:16; Colossians 3). It is a responsibility and a privilege given to every one of us!

Before you start panicking about what this must mean, take another look at that definition of ministry. It doesn't imply some cookie-cutter model of what ministry must be or must look like. There are only two clear requirements: 1) whatever you do, do it for the glory of God, and 2) it must, in some way, further the gospel of Jesus Christ. That doesn't mean you have to preach the Good News; it simply means you are to be a carrier of the Good News—a light that shines the bright hope and love of Jesus Christ everywhere you go. These two requirements are to be fulfilled by showing up where you are and using what you have been given. Ministry, therefore, is as unique as you are and cannot fit into a neat and tidy box with a carefully printed label on top.

In one of her earliest books, Jennie Allen urges her readers to begin seeing their regular, daily lives as opportunities for ministry. These words have remained with me over the years, and I want to share them with you. I want to *commission* you with these words:

> So do your everyday and your ordinary. Godliness is found and formed in those places. No man or woman greatly used by God has escaped them. Great men and women of God have transformed the mundane, turning neighborhoods into mission fields, parenting into launching the next generation of God's voices, legal

work into loving those most hurting, waiting tables into serving and loving in such a way that people see our God.²

The way you show up in your everyday life and use what God has given you, fully leaning into who He made you to be, is the breeding ground of your ministry. It is how you can most effectively and consistently serve and love the people around you. Not so they notice you and give you glory, but that they see God in you and through you. The small, seemingly inconsequential things you do for other people have the power to change their lives because there is something, or someone, bigger at play. Just one single spark can ignite a forest fire. Imagine what one spark of kindness, one spark of God's love shone through you, could do! Who's to say what sparks an awakening, a revival, in someone's life?

Be Where You Are

If the ministry of small things consists of showing up right where we are in life, then it's crucial to acknowledge and accept where we are. But we are often guilty of wallowing in thoughts about *someday* when we get *there*—wherever we think we should be.

When my baby starts sleeping through the night, I'll be able to enjoy motherhood.

When football season (or insert any sport here) is over, we'll start going to church again.

When I get the promotion, then I'll be able to…

When life slows down, I would love to…

When I graduate college or get that job or find a boyfriend/husband or finally have enough followers on social media, I can…

Someday when…

The problem with living for someday—that often elusive day when all the stars align, and life will be exactly as it "should" be—is that it is always out there somewhere. When we think we are about to attain it, to finally have it within our reach, someday slips further into the future.

The job may come, the husband may be found, or the busy season may end, but something else inevitably pops up. While that job may have been what you were striving toward, now you realize it will require more work than you thought. The man of your dreams captured your heart, and now all you can think about is starting a family. You made it out of that wild season of sports and school projects only to find yourself staring at the beginning of the hectic holiday season—school parties, work parties, family gatherings, and all the Christmas presents to buy and wrap.

Living for someday becomes a problem when it is our excuse for not living today—not showing up right where we are. When our eyes and attention are solely set on that time somewhere in the future, our hands and feet can't be grounded in what is right in front of us and what is for us to do today. We neglect to understand that *today*—no matter how small, trivial, or imperfect—is our life. *Today* is where God has placed us and when God has placed us.

Today is your time and place for ministry. Today is what you have to work with. Today matters right now. You don't have to learn more, have more, or be more. Ministry is for every believer, whether you feel qualified or ready or not. Your regular, everyday life right now is where you are positioned to bring glory to God and proclaim the good news of His love. Dallas Willard says it like this:

> First we must accept the circumstances we constantly

find ourselves in as the place of God's Kingdom and blessing. God has yet to bless anyone except where they actually are, and if we faithlessly discard situation after situation, moment after moment, as not being "right," we will simply have no place to receive His Kingdom into our life. For those situations and moments are our life.[3]

How you live your everyday, ordinary life has Kingdom impact. God's Kingdom is found in your regular, routine-filled life. And as Willard says, "God has yet to bless anyone except where they actually are." So, the urge here is to actually *be* where you are—not where you want to be or where you think you should be.

Where are you today?

That's a serious question. Where are you in life right now? Your answer is ground zero for the ministry you are called to and most equipped for today. When you open your groggy eyes in the morning, where are you? Where are the places most traveled by your feet (or car)? Where do you regularly put your hands to work? Who are the people you have access to daily, consistently?

I'm confident there are many more people in your sphere of influence than you can think of right now. Family members and friends. Coworkers, fellow volunteers, team members, teachers, and coaches. Neighbors, the people you usually try to avoid while at the grocery store, your server, barista, store clerk. Your kids' friends and teammates *and* their parents. Or how about the people in your community who are desperate for help? There are homeless shelters, ministries providing food to those in need, programs for mentoring and caring for children, and even the foster care system and adoption agencies filled with children who need homes and people to love them. All of this—all of these people—can be found right where you are. And they need you now—not someday.

So, while you are hoping for, working toward, praying for, and anticipating the future—which is not a bad thing—don't forget to look up and show up today. Find one person today who could use some encouragement. Say a sincere "Hi" to someone at the store and be open to chatting for a few minutes. Put a friendly smile on your face as you go about your errands. You never know what one little action—a smile, a sincere compliment, a single text, an act of kindness—can do in someone else's life. Even the smallest gestures can shed a little hope-filled light in the lives of those who receive them. Your regular, mundane life is where you have been planted to live for the glory of God and the good of His people.

What You Have Been Given

Another aspect of this "small things ministry" is using what you have been given—what you have available to you right now—for the benefit of others and the glory of God. Just as you must recognize where you are, you must also begin to acknowledge and appreciate what you have been given. Whether you believe it or not, you have been given everything you need to effectively walk in the life of ministry to which you are called.

If you grew up going to church or have spent any time in church, you have probably heard at least one sermon on the *Parable of the Talents* found in Matthew 25:14-30. It is a perennial favorite among many pastors and preachers and highly applicable to our lives. We don't have to dig too deep to find wisdom in Jesus's words.

Before we get to the wisdom, here's a quick refresher. While talking to His disciples about the end of the age and the Kingdom of Heaven, Jesus recounts this parable about a master who goes on a long journey. As the man prepares to leave, he summons his servants and gives them each a certain amount of his wealth to steward, or care for, while he is gone. One man receives five talents (a measure of money—we will talk more about this in a minute), another man receives two talents, and another receives one talent.

As the parable goes, the first two men work with what they have been given and make even more. The last man, who received only one talent, digs a hole and buries it, essentially doing nothing with what he had been given. When the master returns, the first two men are celebrated and commended. The final man is not, and what he has is given to the first man instead.

For reference, a talent, or a bag of gold as the New International Version translates it, was "worth about 20 years of a day laborer's wage."[4] Thus, the servants were given 100, 40, and 20 years' worth of wages, respectively. They were supplied with what they would need to live, work, and thrive while their master was away. Even the man with only one talent had been given significant resources.

The question, then, is: What did they do with what they had been given?

The first two men put to work what they had been given. They were not held back by the size of what was entrusted to them. I'd imagine they could have been; they were given large sums of money, after all. What if they were overly concerned about losing it all? What if they had focused more on the outcome than what they were asked to do? Maybe they, too, would have hidden what they had been given.

Perhaps the third man was hindered by the apparent smallness of what was given to him—only one talent, while his fellow servants were given more. What could he possibly do with just this little bit compared to what they could do? Perhaps his focus was on the outcome rather than what he had actually been given and asked to do. (We'll pick up this discussion on the result of what we are asked to do in a later chapter.) His master expected him to put his talent to work and do something with it, but perhaps the third servant couldn't get past what little he had.

It's easy to focus on what we don't have or haven't been given. It takes minimal effort to notice all the things we can't do, all the legs-up we haven't received, and all the "talents" we don't possess—especially in the social media and celebrity-driven world in which we now live. But what if we focus on what we *do* have and what we *can* do instead? All that time feeling down or complaining about what we are missing would be replaced with actually doing what we can do.

The master in Jesus's parable praised the faithfulness of the first two servants, not their success or prosperity. He was pleased by their actions, not their outcomes. The words he spoke to these servants are now well-known: "Well done, good and *faithful* servant. You have been faithful over a little; I will set you over much" (Matthew 25:21, 23 ESV, emphasis added).

The words spoken to the third servant, however, bring me pause today: "You wicked and lazy servant!" (v. 26 NLT). The servant's laziness displeased his master. The servant's lack of effort let his master down. The master wasn't after specific results; he was looking for faithfulness—a servant who stewarded what he had been given.

So, I ask you: What have you been given that you can put to work for the glory of God and the good of others? Yes, this idea holds within it talents and abilities, but it also contains so much more.

THE MINISTRY OF SMALL THINGS

If you can sing, sing for the glory of God. If you can write, write for His glory and to point others to Him. If you can draw, paint, sculpt, or dance, you can do it as worship unto God. If you have free time in your daily schedule, you can fill it with prayer and Bible reading, helping a neighbor in need, feeding the hungry, tutoring kids at your local elementary school, or leading a small group. If you have extra financial resources, you can put them to work helping build the Kingdom of God or meeting someone's immediate needs.

Do you have a job? Do you interact with people daily? Find ways to bring little snippets of God's Kingdom into your workplace and your relationship with others. You may be the only person in someone's life that knows and is living for Jesus. What if you are meant to shine His light in her life?

What have you been given today?

Breath in your lungs.

Words in your mouth.

Fingers to type a hopeful message on social media.

A mouth to smile.

A hand to wave.

Food in your refrigerator.

Warm clothes in your closet.

A job. School. Family.

Time.

You have no lack of resources, especially if you live in the western world. So, the question is: *What will you do with what you have been given?*

What Holds Us Back?

Ministry is right in front of us in our regular, day-to-day lives—the people, the places, the hurting, those in need, and even our family and friends. We don't have to look far or long for people who need to be loved, cared for, prayed over, encouraged, or just simply seen. As we've already discussed, not being where we are and not recognizing what we have already been given can hold us back from fully embracing the ministry of small things. But there is something else that often holds us back, too.

You may be like me, and you have some serious doubts about your ability to show up and use what you have been given. What if you mess up? What if you try to help, and they don't want it? What if you say or do the wrong thing? What if you are just plain wrong? I mean, who really wants anything from you anyway? You've got your own problems, and they will probably see right through you.

When written out like that, it's easier to see the common factor in all those "what ifs."

It's us.

When we are trapped in invisible prisons, erected and fortified by nagging lies and a false understanding of self, we can't see the people, needs, and opportunities around us. Everything is filtered through our guilt, shame, doubt, insecurity, and the list could go on. Before we can move forward with even the regular, day-to-day ministry right before us, we have to break free from what *we think* about ourselves and begin to believe what *God says* about us.

Those thoughts, repeating like broken records in our minds, come from somewhere. Unfortunately, it's been my experience that they can originate with something as simple and little as words spoken to us or about us.

When Words Wound

"How could you ever minister to someone after this?"

"You were used by the devil for his evil plans."

"You must have tempted *him*."

"You have a rebellious spirit."

I teased this back in Chapter 2, not intending to return to it, at least in this book. But here we are. At the abrupt ending of the ministry internship I had joined as an eager and impressionable young adult, I felt as though I was slapped in the face by the words that came out of a leader's mouth.

I have no problem admitting my mistakes that led to being "kicked out" of the internship. I signed up for a year of learning and growing through highly intensive ministry, and I agreed to no dating of any sort during that time. My fellow intern and I failed to uphold our word, and we deserved to be removed from the internship. However, I will not own up to deserving the words spewed at me while being told to gather my things and leave. Accusations were thrown around like confetti, but they hit like tiny explosives, wounding my soul.

Broken, bruised, and entirely lost, I picked up the pieces of my shattered self and did the only thing I knew to do. I carried on. Going home, I moved forward with the plans my *finally official* boyfriend and I had in place. Bible college. Apartments across the hall from each other. Roommates. Life.

A little over a year after that infamous day of dismissal, I married the man with whom I had disgraced the entire ministry internship. The temptress secured her prey. (Just in case it's not clear, please read that with sarcasm.) If they only knew how wrong they were about me…but did *I* know how wrong they were about me?

Words have the power to wound us.

Cruel and careless words screeched at you across the school playground. Harsh and hateful words whispered in your direction in the locker room. Rude and demeaning remarks about your body, hair, or skin. Flippant comments made in passing about your kids or family members. Even rumors make their way back to you about something you may or may not have ever said or done.

Or maybe it's closer than that. Your parents only ever point out your mistakes and shortcomings. Your boyfriend jokingly picks on your appearance. Your friends make fun of something you genuinely like—movies, music, clothes. A teacher or boss questions your intelligence. Your husband echoes criticisms your parents used to throw at you. Or he walks away, shouting without words that you aren't good enough anymore.

That familiar adage, "Sticks and stones may break my bones, but words will never hurt me," couldn't be farther from the truth. Words may not break us on the outside. They may not cause immediate destruction, and they may not be noticeable to anyone else. But words do more than just hurt us. They confuse us, hold us back, and bind us in insecurity, doubt, and sometimes even self-hatred. A physical break we can heal with physical measures, but words don't wound us physically. They hit deeper. They last longer. And they can alter how we live and what we believe about ourselves. No, words are far more dangerous than mere sticks and stones. Wounding words have a way of making us believe them.

When I think back, I'm not surprised it took so many years for the effects of those hazardous and toxic words to surface, revealing the damage left in their wake. For during those early years, the inner turmoil of my heart and soul was masked and overshadowed by life. My husband and I jumped from one life-defining moment to the next with little time and space to breathe for years—graduating from Bible college, having babies, moving houses multiple times, and pursuing full-time ministry. All the while, those shattered pieces of myself I had gathered years before were still rattling around inside, broken and untouched.

Rather than allowing myself to heal, I began to believe what was spoken over me. Not in an overt kind of way. It was discreet and slow, gaining strength over time. I struggled to find friends because I was convinced I had nothing positive to give. Who would possibly want to be my friend and like me for who I am? I fought serious, debilitating thoughts of always being wrong and always having the wrong motivation. I was lonely, scared, and insecure, but I was too broken to admit it to anyone—even myself. Seeing and loving the people around me—other than my husband and children—was pretty much out of the question. What did I have left after spending so much energy trying to protect myself from being hurt again?

I believed the lies that were spoken over me. I thought I was damaged goods, useless to anyone other than my family. For years, I was trapped behind those lies, bound by who I thought I was and who other people told me I was.

But God...

God began a good work in me when He helped me change the way I thought about my life—when He taught me how to find beauty and goodness in the ordinariness of every day. He continued that good work when I began faithfully and humbly showing up to His Word because it was then, and only then, that His truth set me free. When the truth of who He is and who I am because of Him became the guiding light of my life, I finally was able to see what had held me captive for so long. Lies. Hurtful words that held no truth held me hostage in a prison of self-doubt, self-hate, and self-obsession.

Yes, words have the power to wound us, but the Word has the power to heal us. To set us free. To teach us the truth. To guide us along the path of life.

When our insecurities lead us, we only see ourselves. When we are secure in who God is and who He says we are, we are freed up to see, truly see, the people around us—whether that is our children, parents, spouse, coworkers, the cashier at the store, the homeless man on the side of the road, that one person who always rubs us the wrong way, or the people on the other side of the political aisle.

When we get out of our way, when the "what ifs" are no longer strong enough to keep us down, and when we know and believe the truth about ourselves, our eyes and hearts will be opened to the beauty of the ministry of small things. And we'll recognize the profound privilege of being called to and equipped for such ordinary, day-to-day, holy work.

Is It Too Small a Thing?

Where you are right now and what you have in front of you—is it too small? The people and the places of your everyday life—are they not worth what you have to give? Or let's flip it…are you too small, insignificant, or unworthy to make a difference in someone's life today?

The answer to these questions is just as it has been throughout this book. No.

Where you are right now, today isn't just a stepping stone to someday. What you have in front of you and what you have been given are enough to do exactly what you were created to do—to glorify God and share His Good News. And those people and places that fill your days are just as valuable to God as you are. They are worth what God has given you to help them, love them, guide them, cheer them up, or just plain be with them.

And, my friend, you are not too small, too simple, too hidden, too forgotten, too *anything* for God to work through you. Because, remember, it's not really about you anyway. When you show up, you're not showing up for yourself. You're not gathering followers for yourself or people indebted to you. No, no, no. You're merely showing up as a response to the One who first showed up for you without hesitation or regret.

The ministry of small things just may be the biggest ministry any of us could ever hope for. Life is simply the culmination of every little, day-to-day, ordinary thing. If we can faithfully steward the small stuff, maybe the words we all long to hear will ring out at the end of our days: "Well done my good and faithful servant."

Make This Prayer Yours

Lord, I'm sorry for the times I have thought myself too small to do anything for you. I'm sorry for judging others as not worth my time or effort. I'm sorry for when I have complained about where I am—even when it's been hard and ugly. I don't want to live that way anymore. Please open my eyes and heart to the people and places around me who need you—who need truth, hope, a smile, or a simple kind gesture. Open my eyes and heart to the ministry of small things. Help me walk in it. Help me put to work what you have given me—even when I feel like it is not enough. Help me honestly believe that small can be significant. I lean on you, Lord. I put my trust in you. In the name of Jesus, amen.

Notes

1. Robert Hampshire, "What is Ministry?" Christianity.com, March 16, 2020, https://www.christianity.com/wiki/church/what-is-ministry.html.

2. Jennie Allen, *Anything: The Prayer that Unlocked My God and My Soul* (Nashville, Tennessee: W Publishing, 2011), 165.

3. Dallas Willard, *The Divine Conspiracy: Rediscovering Our Hidden Life in God* (London: William Collins, 2014), 381-382.

4. Craig S. Keener, Notes in Matthew, *NIV Cultural Backgrounds Study Bible: Bringing to Life the Ancient World of Scripture* (Craig S. Keener and John H. Walton, eds., Grand Rapids, Michigan: Zondervan, 2016), 1664.

Ruth's Story

The Book of Ruth

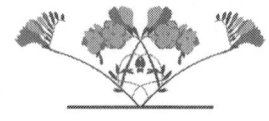

Who am I?

What am I doing?

Why am I here?

Far from home, widowed and childless, Ruth must have questioned, at least once, her decision to leave her family, her home, and everything familiar behind and follow her mother-in-law to her homeland. Ruth was an outsider, after all. She wasn't one of God's people. She didn't know anyone, believe in the same God, or fully understand their customs. But what else did she have…who else did she have?

Ruth and her mother-in-law, Naomi, found themselves in similar situations—both widowed and without sons—leaving them few options for survival and quality of life. Although Ruth was of child-bearing age and could have remarried, she chose to remain with Naomi and live in Bethlehem instead.

For their survival, Ruth gathered leftover grain from the fields. It was strenuous work, requiring her to pick from hard-to-reach places. It was all she could do. Did it feel like enough? She was faithful to her work and her mother-in-law, and she kept at it.

Eventually, the field owner, Boaz, a relative of Naomi's late

RUTH'S STORY

husband, took notice of Ruth, having heard of her commitment to Naomi and her hard work in the field. He offered her safety and protection in the fields and provided water and food for her sustenance. When Naomi heard of what happened, knowing precisely who Boaz was, she concocted a plan.

Ruth, once again, found herself in an unfamiliar place. Following Naomi's instructions, Ruth approached Boaz one night after he had laid down and fallen asleep. She obediently (probably awkwardly, I'd imagine) uncovered his feet and curled up beside them, waiting for him to notice and tell her what to do next.

Who am I?

What am I doing?

Why am I here?

At midnight, Boaz was startled awake. Maybe his feet were cold, or perhaps he felt Ruth's breath on his feet as she slept. "Who are you," he asked (3:9). When Ruth revealed her identity, she must have been relieved he didn't recoil in shock or disfavor. Boaz did the exact opposite. He pledged to care for her.

It's important to note that there are cultural undertones throughout this encounter from which we are thousands of years and miles removed. What seems confusing and mildly inappropriate or strange to us would have made sense at the time.

Boaz was in a position to redeem his relatives, Naomi and Ruth. He could buy their land and lawfully marry Ruth to reestablish the estate of the deceased. However, Boaz knew there was another redeemer closer in relation, and Naomi and Ruth would have been his responsibility first.

Whether out of devotion for Ruth or duty to the family, we may never know, Boaz approached the other man. This man could not fulfill his duty, so Boaz walked away as the rightful redeemer.

Ruth secured a blessed life for herself and Naomi through her loyalty and obedience to her mother-in-law. The journey she began by following Naomi to her hometown turned into a beautiful story of redemption. No longer a childless widow, Ruth found herself in the loving care of a righteous man who gave her a son.

She came as a foreigner without family, but she lived the rest of her days as one who belonged, as one who was loved.

But her story doesn't stop there…

Part 3

Is It Too Small a Thing...
What God is Asking of You?

In the final part of this book, our attention will move toward the missional, or calling, part of life. Here, we focus our favorite question on what God asks of us.

In this section, we will:

- Take a realistic look at how God speaks to us and how we can know what He asks of us.
- Explore the less-celebrated aspect of obedience—not the steps of extraordinary obedience but the small, consistent, and often *unglamorous* steps.
- Discover our part in determining the significance and outcome of what God asks us to do.

What God asks of us, how He asks it, and what He does with it is no small thing. By the end of this part of the book, my goal is for us to believe that—more than before. And, hopefully, for all of us, this is just the beginning!

Chapter 8
A Little Leading Goes a Long Way

"But, God, how do I know if this is something you are asking me to do? It would be really helpful if you could make it obvious in some way. Maybe you could send a message…or a sign…or something?"

I can't tell you how often I have had this conversation with God over the years. My guess is that you, too, have asked similar questions. Sometimes the most challenging part of following God's lead is first recognizing where He is leading us or what He is asking us to do.

Our journey through life and along the path of faithfulness would be remarkably more straightforward if we always knew the way—if His directions were as clear as "turn right at the next stop sign, follow the road for three miles, and then take a quick left." More often than not, though, His leading is as little and subtle as a whisper or nudge—easy to miss, overlook, or reason away.

In this chapter, we will take a very practical approach toward a better understanding of God's leading in our life—how He guides us, speaks to us, and encourages us along our journey. Spoiler alert: Pay attention to the small things.

Is This What God is Asking Me to Do?

From the moment I began writing this book, I've been itching to tell you a story—the story of how God led me to, well, write this book.

If we were sitting on my couch, cozied up with a blanket and warm drinks in our hands (coffee for you, I'm guessing, and tea for me), then I'd give you the extended version. But, for now, let's say I lost count of how many conversations I had with God about writing this book. They started the same way: "God, is this what you are asking me to do? Is this book an idea from you?"

In 2019, the significance of small things in Scripture and life jumped out at me like never before. Every time I sat down to study the Bible, this theme showed up. I began tracking in a notebook all the "small doesn't mean insignificant" moments in the Bible. And God slowly revealed how this *little* truth had played out in my personal life (and was continuing to play out). He was plowing the soil and planting seeds, which needed plenty of time and space to grow their roots.

In the shower one morning, I wondered if God had been giving me content for a book. I almost jumped out of the water while conditioning my hair as an outline began to take shape. I didn't want to forget it. The question (our favorite question we've been asking this entire book), the three sections, and even the initial title came spilling out. As soon as I was sufficiently clean and conditioned, I quickly dried off and began typing notes into my phone. Thus began the long period of questioning God and

A LITTLE LEADING GOES A LONG WAY

questioning myself.

Was this His idea or my idea?

I questioned my motivation. I questioned how. I questioned when. I questioned everything. I wanted to know *He* was leading me, not my ambition or selfish desires.

In 2021, after a life-defining decision (which you'll hear more about in the following chapters) and many months of seeking God, something happened that convinced me to pull out the index cards and begin putting pen to paper. It wasn't a booming, audible voice. It wasn't a vision of God urging me to sit down and start writing. It was one conversation with a stranger who had no idea about my inner wrestling with God.

Our family car—a minivan, ahem—was totaled that summer on our way to the beach for our family vacation. Everyone was okay, but our beloved Honda Odyssey was not. We are a debt-free car-buying family; unfortunately, our totaled minivan wasn't worth much. So, buying a new (to us) car was a huge deal. We found the right car at the right price and even had a great experience with the salesman. Thank goodness!

When we were ushered into the financial office to sign all the papers, I wondered what God was up to. Something bigger was at play. The Finance Manager learned that my husband was a pastor, and he quickly began opening up to us. In the past month, he had helped seven or so pastors purchase new cars, which was rare according to him. As a result, he found himself encouraged and emboldened to share what he sensed God was asking him to do.

Do you want to know what God was inviting him to do?

He, this perfect stranger, was writing a book about how God

had changed his life.

He told us stories of people who had crossed his path, encouraging him to keep writing. He had one experience after another of being in the right place at the right time for God to use him to help people in need. As he told us story after story, he kept saying how easy it would have been to miss what God wanted him to do and simply not answer His call.

I didn't tell him about the book I was praying about writing. He had no idea. But I walked away heartened, inspired, and, honestly, flabbergasted by our conversation. What are the odds of that happening?

About a week later, while my kids were at Vacation Bible School, which means the house was quiet for the first time all summer, I finally pulled out some color-coded index cards and began plotting out this book (affectionately known at that time as the "small book"). I remembered the conversation I had with the Financial Manager, but I couldn't remember his name. I'm not sure why it mattered at that moment, but it did. He had given us his business card before we left that day, and I had stashed it in our glove box in our new car. So, I dashed outside, pulled out all the manuals and paperwork, and found his card.

Now, this is so random that I can't think of any other way to explain it except: *but God*.

I flipped over his business card so that I could see his information. And right there, in blue ink, his last name was… *Small*. Small!

It might have been a coincidence—an oddly specific coincidence. Or maybe, just maybe, it was a little nudge God providentially orchestrated. Sure, it was a *small* thing, but I'm entirely convinced that small doesn't mean insignificant. And what better way for God to grab my attention than with something quite literally Small?

I finally had the answer to the question I had been asking for years. This book was God's idea. The "small doesn't mean insignificant" message was what God wanted me to explore and tease out for whoever would eventually read this book. *Is it too small a thing?* That wasn't just a catchy question; it was God's question of the moment. And I believe it *still* is.

God, Is That You?

In John 10, Jesus draws a poignant picture of the relationship between a shepherd—the Good Shepherd—and his sheep. He reveals how the shepherd loves, cares for, guides, and, ultimately, will die for His sheep. Notably, Jesus does not have to explain the role of a shepherd nearly as much as would be required today because the first-century way of life was primarily agricultural. What He does emphasize, however, is His identity. "I am the good shepherd," He proclaims, making it clear that His followers are, therefore, the sheep (vs. 11, 14).

In this illustration, not only does Jesus reveal Himself as the Good Shepherd, but He also provides comfort and confirmation for those of us who have ever wondered whether we can actually know when He is leading us. According to the Good Shepherd Himself, His sheep can hear and know His voice, enabling them to follow Him. Familiarity with His voice ensures His sheep will not follow a stranger (vs. 3-5). What a beautiful truth. We can know His voice! He even repeats it in case we didn't get it the first time: "My sheep hear my voice, and I know them, and they follow me" (v. 27 ESV).

So, what does this mean for us? Should we expect to audibly hear the voice of our loving and kind Good Shepherd? I can't give a definitive answer to whether His voice will be audible in your life or not because I'm not God. It's not up to me to decide that. I will give a resounding "yes" to the fact that He still speaks today. He speaks to us through His Word, His people, and His Spirit—all of which will always be in agreement with His Word, by the way. As Dallas Willard writes, "The God who hears is also one who speaks. He has spoken and is still speaking...He continues to speak in ways that serious inquirers can hear if they will."[1]

Let's explore three areas through which we can expect God to speak to us. The more we talk about God speaking to and leading us, the less unexpected and foreign it becomes. After all, God's voice should be the most comforting, familiar, and influential voice we know.

1. God Speaks Through His Word

Do you know about King Josiah in the Bible? His life story is one of my favorites in all of Scripture. (Please forgive me if you ever hear me talking about any other favorite people in the Bible; it's nearly impossible to choose!) You can read about him in 2 Kings 22-23 and 2 Chronicles 34-35.

King Josiah became king at the age of eight. (Can you imagine your eight-year-old reigning over any kingdom other than the one he built out of Legos and toy dinosaurs?) King Josiah was one of the final kings of God's people in the Old Testament and one of the few *good* kings who "did what was right in the eyes of the Lord" (2 Kings 22:2 ESV). He ushered in a great revival among God's people, calling them back to the ways of their ancestors and the holy ways of God.

A LITTLE LEADING GOES A LONG WAY

For generations, God had been calling His people back to Him and requiring the destruction of their false gods and idols. King Josiah took drastic measures to ensure that this happened during his reign. All temples and places to worship other gods were destroyed. He demolished idols and every evil thing keeping the people's lives and hearts from returning to God. Not only that, but he also reinstated laws and mandates God had put into place back in the time of Moses.

It was unlike any other king had done before, resulting in a time of great renewal and awakening for God's people. Unfortunately, the revival didn't last long after King Josiah's death—a tragedy you will have to read about for yourself.

Something sparked this revival. Something guided it. God used *something* to speak to Josiah, leading him to radically alter his life and the life of his people. What was that something? It was the Law of God, their Scripture at this time.

As a young king, Josiah had commissioned the restoration of the Temple—God's holy place of worship built in King Solomon's time. During repairs, the "Book of the Law" was found (leaving us only to assume how long it had been unread, untouched, and forgotten). When King Josiah heard everything written within the Law, his reaction was immediate and visceral, tearing his clothes and weeping before God. He was awakened to all that God had done and all that their ancestors had *not* done. They had not obeyed their God. They had not lived according to His ways. King Josiah repented and turned wholeheartedly back to His God and His ways.

The Word of God guided this change and led King Josiah forward.

It is not different for us today. 2 Timothy 3:16 tells us, "All Scripture is breathed out by God and profitable for teaching, for reproof, for correction, and for training in righteousness." As Bible-believing Christians, this is a foundational truth upon which we build our lives. The Word of God is inspired by God for the express purpose of guiding us in His truth and His ways. That's what it did for King Josiah; it revealed where they were wrong and what must be corrected. And that's what it does for us today.

God leads us through His Word. God speaks to us through His Word. The book we have the privilege of holding in our hands and flipping open whenever we desire is the guiding voice for our lives! It is the foremost way God leads His people today.

2. **God Speaks Through His People**

The story of Esther in the Old Testament is pivotal within the greater story of God's people. If you have ever read it—the entire book of Esther is only ten chapters—you may have noticed no mention of God whatsoever. No prayer. No worship. No Law. Yet, "God seems to lurk everywhere in the background of this book, in the unlikely coincidences and remarkable deliverances."[2] And through it all, God speaks—even though there are no "thus sayeth the Lords." God speaks through one particular person who helps guide and direct Esther through a life-and-death situation.

Here's a quick rundown. Esther is a Jew living with

her uncle, Mordecai, in the Persian empire. (The Persians had conquered the Babylonians, who had conquered and taken captive Esther's ancestors, God's people—the Jews.) Through a rather dramatic series of events, Esther becomes Queen of Persia—honestly, the ordeal resembles a season of *The Bachelor*. However, as advised by Mordecai, Esther never reveals her true identity as a Jew. Even though God is not mentioned in this book, it is obvious the amount of divine favor in which Esther walks.

Eventually, one of the king's highest officials devises a plot to annihilate all the Jews in the Persian empire. Mordecai informs Esther of this sinister plan, convincing her of the responsibility that she alone holds for her people—that perhaps she had been entrusted with her royal position "for such a time as this" (4:14). Trusting his wisdom and guidance, Esther devises a plot of her own—a plot that eventually saves her people and destroys their enemies instead.

God's guidance is undeniable throughout this book, and much of it comes from the mouth of Mordecai. His wisdom and knack for being at the right place at the right time directly affect the fate of Esther and their people.

The lack of direct involvement or acknowledgment of God is considered to be intentional by most scholars. The book of Esther reads similar to how we would interpret our own lives—an undercurrent of God's guidance through people in our lives without any explicit "thus sayeth the Lords."

This is not to say that God will speak through everyone in our lives or that we should seek His voice in every encounter. Remember what Jesus says of His sheep: They will know His voice and will not follow the voice of a stranger. There is a difference, and we can recognize the difference. Praise God! The more familiar we are with His voice through His Word, the more familiar we will be with His voice through His people. Because His voice—His guidance and leading—will never contradict His Word.

3. **God Speaks Through His Spirit**
   Getting right down to it, each of the ways God speaks that we have discussed so far falls into this category of God speaking through His Spirit, or the Holy Spirit, for it is the voice of the Holy Spirit that speaks to us through the Word and other people. The Holy Spirit *is* God—let's make that clear! For our understanding, however, it helps to have the categories of God speaking through His Word and His people.

   Jumping into the topic of the Holy Spirit could be a book in and of itself.[3] However, for our purposes, I will carefully and just barely brush the topic.

   In John 16, as Jesus talks to His disciples about leaving, He comforts them with the revelation of the Holy Spirit. He declares it will be better for them (and us) when He leaves because it is only then that He can send the Holy Spirit—the helper, advocate, comforter, counselor, and teacher (vs. 6-7). The Holy Spirit will speak to them, Jesus says. The Holy Spirit will guide them and tell them what they will need to know from God the Father (v. 13).

The Holy Spirit still does these things for us today. Sometimes His voice comes through the Word of God, sometimes His voice comes through other people, and sometimes His voice comes through something else.

One frequent description of the Holy Spirit's guidance is that of a whisper. Perhaps it comes from an account in the Old Testament in which Elijah, a great prophet, searches for the Lord. Elijah endures earth-shattering wind, an earthquake, and fire—each very powerful, but the Lord is not found in any of it. In the near silence of a low whisper, however, Elijah finds the Lord. When Elijah hears that still, small voice, he knows it is the Lord and is overcome by the power of it (1 Kings 19:11-13).

A whisper. God's power was found in a whisper. God's voice was heard in a whisper.

Is God whispering in your life? Are you quiet enough to hear it? Are you close enough? That's the thing about a whisper—you must be close to hear it. It's intimate. It's tender.

A whisper implies proximity. Not just on your part but on God's part, too. God is as close as the tiniest whisper. His closeness is only possible through the Holy Spirit—here with me and there with you at all times.

God speaks through the Holy Spirit—the still, small voice. And He will "guide [us] into all the truth"—that's what Jesus tells us (John 16:13 ESV). Are you listening?

The Psalm 37:4 Test

If you have ever asked a friend or spiritual leader how to know when God is asking you to do something specific, the responses were probably one or all of these: pray, seek God, and spend time in the Word. All necessary and appropriate. But maybe it was a bit discouraging because you were already doing those things. Perhaps you wanted a different answer—a more practical answer.

I get that because I have been there, too!

We *should* pray, seek God, and spend time in His Word when we are trying to discern the will of God for a situation or a dream or desire. Rather than walking away discouraged from that advice, I'd like to help you see it in a different light—just as God helped me quite a few years ago.

I tend to call this the Psalm 37:4 Test. Psalm 37:4 says, "Delight yourself in the Lord, and He will give you the desires of your heart" (ESV). Maybe you've seen a coffee mug plastered with these words. Or a journal. Or a framed print. It's a hopeful, promising Scripture to lean on and take hold of! In fact, I have a locket inscribed with Psalm 37:4 that I used to wear every day.

To keep this as simple as possible, let me ask two questions. According to this verse, *what is our part to do?* We are to "delight" in the Lord. To "delight" in the Lord is to spend time with Him, to *want* to know Him, and love Him. Another way to say it is to pray (talk to Him), seek Him (spend time with Him), and read His Word (get to know Him). It's the advice we are usually given, right?

Now, *what will God do?* The verse says He will give us the desires of our hearts. What if rather than God merely granting our desires as we learn to know Him and trust Him, He actually establishes the desires within us? He puts the desires there as we spend time delighting in Him.

Let's take a peek into the original Hebrew for a minute.

The Hebrew word translated as "delight" in this verse is defined as "to be soft, delicate, dainty."[4] That doesn't initially fit with *our* definition of delight, does it? Well, think about what happens as we intentionally spend time with God—as we pray and seek Him and study His Word to better know Him. Hopefully, we become more soft and tender toward Him and His ways. We become like malleable clay in the hands of the infinitely adept Potter.

Yes, He gives us our desires as we delight in Him. But because we are delighting in Him—spending time with Him and conforming to His ways—our desires will be His desires. This is how we can stand on the promise that He will give us the desires of our hearts because they are His desires, too.

So, when we are trying to discern whether God is asking us to do something specific, we should ask: *Am I delighting in Him?* It's like an assessment test. If we can honestly say we have been spending time in His presence, praying, and reading His Word, then we would have strong reason to believe the desire or idea is from Him. Simply put: If you have a dream or desire or idea, something you want to do or sense God is leading you to do, and it persists even as you continue delighting in Him, then maybe it's time for you to go for it!

Understanding Psalm 37:4 in this way has changed how I pursue ideas and dreams, even though I often have to remind myself of its truth. If I am tending to my personal relationship with my Good Shepherd, then I can trust Him to tend to my heart and the ideas, dreams, and desires that flow from it. Aside from Mr. Small's business card, the fact that the desire to write this book persisted for years—as I dug deeper into God's Word and as I began to pray and seek Him more intentionally—has convinced me it is God's idea. It passed the Psalm 37:4 test.

Do you have dreams and desires that have persisted as you've delighted in the Lord? What about that one thing you always wanted to do? It never seems to go away. It's in the back of your mind, slowly tapping to ensure you don't forget it's there. It pops up from time to time as you pray or as you find yourself in a good spot with the Lord. Or maybe you are reminded of it as you encourage others in their dreams.

Like me, you've always wanted to write a book.

Or you can't stop thinking about going back to school.

Or that idea for a new business just keeps popping up.

Or maybe it's something you keep thinking about doing for or saying to someone.

It's just there all the time. You pray about it, and it persists. It creeps in as you are worshiping or reading your Bible. It may feel random or not make sense, but what if God is behind the helm, wanting to lead you forward?

It sounds like that thing, whatever it is, just might pass the Psalm 37:4 Test. Maybe it's time to step out and do the thing, trusting that God will lead the way forward.

Sometimes You Just Know (Without Actually Knowing)

There were a couple of things my husband and I *knew* since

the beginning of our relationship. One, we were committed to loving God and following His lead—even though the way our relationship began could have easily convinced us we would fail at that. And two, we believed we were called to vocational ministry in the local church. In fact, our deepest desire was to plant and pastor a church.

We tended to our church-planting dream for over a decade as my husband faithfully worked outside the church, continuing even as he became a pastor at our local church. In the early years, we pursued training and prepared ourselves the best we knew how, waiting for God's timing and His greenlight to go. Waiting and trusting—that's what characterized those years the most.

One night, we went to dinner with a couple preparing to do the very thing we wanted to do. They were packing up their lives, moving to a new city, and launching a new church. We had received similar training, attended the same conferences, and learned from the same ministry leaders. And all of the advice was the same: Plant churches in big cities. Go to the urban areas. Find the masses of people and plant there. Big cities lead to big launches. Big launches lead to big churches.

Throughout our dinner, I couldn't shake the feeling that the "big approach" to planting a church didn't feel right for us. I was too embarrassed to admit that I couldn't see myself living in an urban environment. Was I wrong to desire the slowness of a smaller town and maybe even a smaller church? It was the opposite of everything we were discussing and everything we had learned.

That conversation stuck with me for years. While the conversation stuck, the feelings of being wrong or embarrassed didn't. Our idea of success as a church and church planters was being reshaped by the Teacher Himself.

Fast forward several years (emphasis on several), my husband, firmly planted and flourishing as a pastor at the same local church, and I, growing in all the ways I've discussed in the book up to this point, began to sense God's timing drawing near. While we were unsure of what that meant, we were trying to be attentive to His guidance. And one morning, that leading came in the form of our pastor. He approached Jamie, my husband, with the idea of launching a new campus of our church. He wanted Jamie to lead it, and, here's the kicker, he believed the location was to be a very small town thirty miles away.

Jamie walked in the door that afternoon, practically bursting with the news. Of course, nothing had been decided other than needing to pray about the decision for a few days. It would be a bold move for our church and a life-changing decision for our family. However, Jamie and I agreed almost immediately that this was what we were supposed to do.

Years before, my gravitation toward a small town seemed misguided amid all the fixation on large cities. But I came to realize that was the ever-so-gentle whisper of the Holy Spirit. I just needed time to recognize it. What once seemed random and opposite of what I should have thought now revealed itself as confirmation of the plan God had intended all along.

Is It Too Small a Thing?

You know how this goes by now… Is it too small a thing how God decides to lead us? His whisper, nudge, and gentle way of guiding us—is it too small? Those little things that pop up, the few words from a stranger or trusted friend, or the words of Scripture—are they too small or insignificant to be God's voice in our lives?

No! You knew that would be the answer, huh?

A LITTLE LEADING GOES A LONG WAY

The more I live this life, the more I learn about God, and the more I know His voice, the more I'm convinced that small things matter. The small ways God directs our thoughts and actions. Those few words someone uses to encourage us. The nudge of the Spirit that just won't go away. The Scripture we read today that sparked something in us.

It's easy to explain away or overlook much of how God leads us and speaks to us. We live in an age that values science, evidence, and reason. If we can't prove it, we don't want to believe it. But isn't that what faith is? Believing in something—someone—you can't physically, scientifically prove. Hebrews 11:1 gives us this definition: "Now faith is the substance of things hoped for, the evidence of things not seen" (KJV). Faith is confident of that which cannot be seen, measured, or proven scientifically.

Recognizing and trusting the leading of God requires faith—faith to acknowledge it and faith to follow it. While it may be tempting and, honestly, more comfortable to brush His little nudges, His whisper, and those divine "coincidences" off as anything but divine, remember how God has shown up time and time again in the Bible. Yes, we hear Him in the "thus sayeth the Lords" of the Old Testament prophets, but we hear Him even more often in the little, quiet, and sometimes ordinary occurrences of everyday life. It was the reading of the Law for Josiah. It was the guidance of Mordecai for Esther. It was the hush of the whisper for Elijah. Not a big audible voice. Not a thundering, earthquaking moment. Not a prophetic voice. (Not that I'm saying it can't be!)

Take notice of the small things, friend. It just may be how your big, infinite Good Shepherd has decided to guide you. And be encouraged that as His sheep, you *can* know and follow His voice—however and through whomever He chooses to speak.

Make This Prayer Yours

Lord, I'm sorry for the times I have been too busy, distracted, or loud to hear you. I want to know your voice like you promise I can. I want to be familiar with your voice and only follow you. For that, I need your help. Help me learn your voice, help me follow your ways, and help me turn from the voice of a stranger. Help me be open to and aware of how you speak in my life. It's easier to notice big moments, but I know you are also in the small moments. You are with me every day! And just as I know you hear me, help me remember that you also respond! In the name of Jesus, amen.

Notes

1. Dallas Willard, *The Divine Conspiracy: Rediscovering Our Hidden Life in God* (London: William Collins, 2014), 41.

2. John H. Walton, Introduction to Esther, *NIV Cultural Backgrounds Study Bible: Bringing to Life the Ancient World of Scripture* (Craig S. Keener and John H. Walton, eds., Grand Rapids, Michigan: Zondervan, 2016), 801.

3. Two helpful and informative books about the Holy Spirit: *Delighting in the Trinity* by Michael Reeves and *Forgotten God* by Francis Chan.

4. Strong's Hebrew: 6026. עָנַג (ANOG) -- to be soft, delicate, dainty. Accessed February 12, 2023. https://biblehub.com/hebrew/6026.htm.

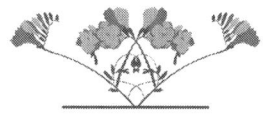

Chapter 9
One Obedient Step at a Time

I'm going to make a generalization. Ready for it?

We like big moments. We like the climax of the story. We want to read about, watch, and be entertained by other people's mountaintop moments. (We also tend to relish in peoples' valleys, too. What can I say? We're complex.) The nearly insurmountable odds. The seemingly impossible. The things we wish we could do. It is inspiring; it gets our blood pumping and our dreams soaring.

In the Christian life, noteworthy and celebrated accomplishments are often highlighted as moments of extraordinary obedience. Impressive obedience is praised and touted as the goal all believers should strive for. Do the next "big thing" for God. Take that huge leap of faith. Sell it all and move halfway around the world. The standard becomes obedience that requires everything you have to give. Obedience that turns heads. Obedience that gets the prayers and public support.

As a result, this biblically central theme of obedience is often undervalued and even unexplored in the everyday lives of everyday people. But for those who are genuinely interested in living according to God's ways, obedience is unavoidable and so much more than those mountaintop, praiseworthy moments. First, this kind of living requires the understanding that life is a series of small, daily, obedient steps made in the same direction. (Thank you, Eugene Peterson.[1]) Second, it requires discipline and character to walk it out, to take that one small, obedient step at a time. Those small, obedient steps become the bulk of life, and sometimes they just might lead to a moment of inspiring, extraordinary obedience.

You see, moments of extraordinary obedience rarely happen without a well-tested, well-proven history of entirely ordinary obedience—obedience of the everyday, regular, day-in and day-out variety. Unspectacular and often unnoticed by the masses, but completely faithful and noticed by the One to whom the obedience actually belongs.

Getting to the Heart of It

Let's start plain and simple. What *is* obedience? In the strictest sense of the word, obedience is about following a command—doing what you are told to do. Other words that may come to mind are compliance, submission, and conformity. Or, often with our kids, for example, we ask them to *mind* us, to *mind* their teachers, and to *mind* the rules. In this sense, obedience requires action, often leading us to assume our attitude and thoughts are irrelevant in the process.

Biblically, however, obedience involves and requires more than mere action. It isn't about simply minding rules or complying with God's authority. Obedience is less a requirement and expectation and more a response. It's a response to our big God and His big, gracious, long-standing, far-reaching plan. It's a response to who

He is and what He has done for us.

It's not unusual to view our acts of obedience—following the commands of Jesus and minding the rules—as a way to earn God's attention, His pleasure, His favor, His mercy, or you name it. The train of thought may go something like this: If I do this, God will… If I am better or do better, God will save me, or I will have done enough to earn salvation. It's easy, then, to regard obedience as another thing we have to do.

But, when we begin to know God as He has revealed Himself through His Word—not how we think He is, assume He is, or have been told He is—and when we more fully understand what He has done for us (remember chapters two and three?), obedience becomes our appropriate and even natural response. What else could we do for the One who has done it all for us? What once may have felt like a "have to" shifts in our hearts to a "get to." Because of who God is and what He has done for us, we get to follow Him, obey Him, and try to live our everyday lives in a way that pleases Him. Our whole lives become worship and praise and thanks to Him.

To get straight to the heart of the matter, obedience is just that—a matter of the heart. True, worshipful obedience flows out of a heart steeped in the love and knowledge of God. Pure, grateful obedience is motivated by a heart tethered to the heart of God Himself. Daily, life-surrendering obedience is the natural response of a heart fully surrendered to the Creator and Sustainer of life itself.

Obedience is not a thing to attain or a means to an end; it is the very way of life in which we are meant to walk. It *is* the path of faithfulness. In 1 John 2, we are told, "Those who obey God's word truly show how completely they love him. That is how we know we are living in him. Those who say they live in God should live their lives as Jesus did" (vs. 5-6 NLT). Obedience is following the example of Jesus Christ, living like He did. When we begin to intentionally live a life of obedience, we engage in the process by which we become more and more like Him. Therefore, the core of the Christian life is learning to live a life of daily, repeated, and ongoing obedience.

What has God asked you to do that you continue brushing off as too little or silly? As you read God's Word, what keeps jumping out at you as something you should do…or stop doing?

I believe that even now, the Holy Spirit is at work, nudging you about something—bringing something to your mind. If you are anything like me, you may be tempted to brush it off as too small, too random, or too silly to matter. But, friend, when we truly grasp the heart of obedience, nothing, seriously not a thing, is too small for us to do for our great and mighty King. Every little thing, every trivial thing, every silly thing—if He asks it—is significant.

Walking in love with your nosy neighbor, smiling and waving at the very least—significant.

Choosing kindness and patience at the doctor's office, the DMV, or in line at the grocery store—significant.

Listening to that little nudge and sending an encouraging text to someone who randomly pops into your mind—significant.

Doing the right thing when it would be easy to get away with blurring the line a bit—significant.

Showing up when you don't feel like it—significant.

Saying yes when God says yes and no when God says no—significant.

Waking up thirty minutes early to read your Bible—significant.

Praying in your car on the way to work—significant.

Obeying God in the smallest of things—significant.

In the end, the Christian life isn't so much about *what* God asks you to do but *who* you become while you do it. It's not about doing the things to get somewhere; it's about doing the things to become someone—or better yet, to become *like* someone. Jesus.

Obedience Speaks Louder Than Words

When my now-teenaged son was a preschooler, he liked to test his limits. He was born with an extra dose of passion, and he expressed it in a variety of, let's say, creative ways. Most of the time, he was contained at home, where his energy and exuberance could roam freely (within reason). However, one particular time, while we were not at home, he decided to see how much freedom he could enjoy.

While I was trying on a pair of shoes at the mall, my son, with all the speed his three- or four-year-old self could muster, decided to run out of the store. I mean, he booked it! He ran straight into a large crowd of people, making a beeline for the escalator heading downstairs. Of course, I couldn't catch up with him with one shoe on and one off, and my not-so-gentle commands to "stop" and "come back here" didn't hit their mark. In fact, he turned his head and gave me a big ol' smile when he heard my voice. Luckily, my mom was with me that day, and she was able to catch up with him before he made his way onto the escalator and out of our sight.

Running out of the store and into a crowd of people was a wrong choice he made that day. But for me, as the parent, that wasn't what I was most concerned about. I had come to anticipate his passionate and rash decisions as a young tyke, not that I condoned them. He was a child with plenty of energy to spare! The bigger concern was his lack of obedience, especially when his safety could have been at risk. He thought I was trying to restrict his freedom and his fun, but, in reality, I was trying to keep him safe. Granted, he was young and still figuring out the wide world around him by pushing his boundaries and testing those limits, but we all learned some important lessons that day. Most notably, I discovered obedience would be a sticking point for many years to come.

As our children have grown and our discussions about obedience have rightfully developed alongside them, I have learned that obedience speaks much louder than any words ever could. When my not-so-little children struggle with obeying their father or me, I wonder whether they truly know, love, and trust us. Because if they did, I hope they would understand that what we ask of them is ultimately for their good and well-being (at least as we see it with our limited understanding).

If our children's obedience can speak so loudly, then I think our obedience as God's children also speaks loudly. In fact, I would go so far as to say our obedience to God reveals more about us than we naturally assume…and maybe even more than we prefer. Let's take a closer look at what our obedience communicates about us.

1. Obedience Reveals Our Knowledge of God

The structure of this book is very intentional. Part One, as you will remember, is entirely about our big God, His big plan, and the big hope we have as a result. I couldn't start anywhere else because He is the beginning of everything. Having a proper understanding and perspective of our vast and gracious God determines how we perceive everything else—our lives, our stories, our calling, our dreams and desires, our fears…all of it.

So, when we start talking about obedience, we are, hopefully, coming to this conversation with the proper perspective of who God is, what He has done, and why He would ask of us what He does. Our knowledge of God informs our willingness to obey Him, and, in turn, our obedience reveals what we know about Him.

When we do something out of obedience that might not make sense to our limited understanding, we communicate that we know God's thoughts and ways are far above ours (Isaiah 55:8-9).

When we step out, even though we're unsure and anxious about our ability, we declare that God's grace and ability are all we need and that His power is no match for our weakness, fear, or anxiety (2 Corinthians 12:9)!

When we do those little, seemingly insignificant things, surrounded by a world that may scoff at and belittle us, we acknowledge that we know God sees and honors our faithfulness, especially when others do not (Matthew 25:10; Luke 16:10).

If we truly know and believe God is the God of Genesis 1:1—the One who created the heavens and the earth out of nothing—then there wouldn't be anything we wouldn't do for Him. If we truly know and believe God is the God of Romans 8:38-39—from whose love we cannot and will never be separated—then we would do whatever He asks of us, never fearing what others may think. If we truly know and believe God is the God of Genesis 50:20—who can turn every evil thing into something good for His people—then we would jump at the privilege of having a part to play in His big plan.

When we obey whatever He asks of us, we demonstrate how much we know about our God.

2. **Obedience Reveals Our Love for God**
This revelation comes straight and repeatedly from the mouth of Jesus in John 14 (ESV):

Verse 15 - If you love me, you will keep my commandments.

Verse 21 - Whoever has my commandments and keeps them, he it is who loves me.

Verse 23 - If anyone loves me, he will keep my word.

Verse 24 - Whoever does not love me does not keep my words.

I mentioned this in Chapter 6, but we'll look deeper here. At the end of John 14, Jesus gives us our most convincing proof that our obedience does declare our love for God. Jesus says to His disciples, "The ruler of this world is coming. He has no claim on me, but I do as the Father has commanded me, so that the world may know that I love the Father" (v. 30, 31 ESV).

Don't just read right by that! Jesus—all man and all God—tells His disciples that the enemy, the ruler of this world, is coming. And just in case anyone is wondering, Jesus clarifies that the enemy is no match for Him. The enemy—Satan or the devil or whatever we want to call him—has zero claim on the life of Jesus. None. But Jesus says: I will obey my Father. I will do what He has asked me to do. I will do this thing that is far beneath me. I will let the enemy think he is going to win. I will give my life. I will obey *so the world knows* I *love* my Father.

When we follow His lead and do what He asks us to do—even if we're scared, even if we'd rather not, even if there's something else we'd prefer to do—we are putting His desires first. We prefer Him over ourselves, our comfort, and our desires, and that is love. Love prefers.

Our obedience is an outward show of our love for God. We can sing all day long of our love for Him. We can tell everyone we meet how much we love Him. But even more than that, our obedience declares our love for Him in a way our words never could.

3. **Obedience Reveals Our Trust in God**
Have you ever done a trust fall? I'm not talking about standing in front of a couple of friends and half-heartedly leaning backward until you feel their hands on you. I'm not talking about a trust fall in which your feet remain firmly planted on the ground, knowing you are safe the whole time. I'm talking about an actual trust *fall*—one in which you literally fall, feet up and head back, into the waiting arms of people *beneath* you.

Sometimes that is what it feels like when we obediently follow the Lord—jumping and stepping out into the unknown and trusting that He will be there.

God may lead us in ways that do not make sense to us or the people around us. He may ask us to do something that we would not normally do on our own. Following God through all the terrain and seasons of life isn't guaranteed to be easy. While we aren't promised easy, smooth sailing, we are promised something even better.

In John 16, Jesus warns His disciples that life may not meet their expectations. He challenges them with the risk of death, heartache, trials, and sorrow, yet He offers peace through it all. "I have said these things to you, that in me you may have peace," Jesus tells them. "In the world you will have tribulation. But take heart; I have overcome the world" (v. 33 ESV). Jesus compels them to trust that their *peace* is found in Him—no matter what it may feel or look like around them.

This peace Jesus promises is not a comfortable, soft, and quiet kind of peace. It does not guarantee a physically serene life where everything goes our way. The peace we have in Jesus is "the tranquil state of a soul assured of its salvation through Christ, and so fearing nothing from God and content with its earthly lot, of whatsoever sort that is."[2] This peace is internal and eternal for those in Christ. This peace is knowing that God is there, waiting to catch us as we step out into the life in which He leads us—whatever that may look like.

When we obey God—no matter the circumstances, possible outcomes, or uncertainty—we reveal our trust in Him. We proclaim our conviction that His peace is enough. We take that backward step off the ledge, trusting Him to catch us as we fall.

Obedience won't always feel like a trust fall—please don't think that is what I am saying. But it does and will require the same kind of trust.

While the words we say to and about our God are unmistakably significant, our obedience and actions end up shouting with the most force. When we step out, we make it known just how much we know, love, and trust our God. We declare it to Him, the world, and ourselves.

Why Would God Ask *Me* to Do Anything?

There is no shortage of examples of people from Scripture who learned, sometimes the hard way, the significance and necessity of obedience. We could examine how Abraham's journey of learning to obey God spanned decades and culminated in his willingness to sacrifice his son, for whom he had waited all those decades. We could talk about how it was a tiny thing—striking a rock when he wasn't supposed to—that kept Moses from entering the Promised Land, even though he faithfully, obediently led God's people step by step through the desert for forty years. We could even pick apart the story of the little shepherd boy, David, who listened as God directed him to grab his slingshot and pick up five small stones to defeat the giant, Goliath. Trust me, I could keep going, but this book would end up much longer than it should be. I mean, I *do* want you to finish it!

However, there is one account in the New Testament that I do want to share with you. It stands out because it is, chronologically, the first recorded miracle of Jesus. You can find all the details in John 2, but you may be already familiar with this story.

Jesus is at a wedding. His mother is there, too, along with some of His disciples. We don't have much information about the wedding itself, but we do know weddings could last for days at a time. Culturally, hospitality is highly valued, honored, and expected, which, in turn, means any crisis or unfortunate incident could adversely affect the reputation of the family responsible. So, running out of wine mid-celebration, for example, could disgrace a newlywed couple.

When Jesus is compelled by his mother to do something about the dwindling supply of wine, we get a glimpse of so much more than Jesus merely turning water into wine. In fact, because this is the first miracle of Jesus, I believe God reveals how He often chooses to do what He does. Jesus turns to the servants—those serving the guests of the wedding feast—and invites them into what He is about to do.

Here's how it goes down. There are six water jars, made entirely out of stone, nearby. Each one could hold twenty to thirty gallons of water. When Jesus asks the servants to fill the jars with water, they fill each one "up to the brim" (v. 7 ESV). Keep in mind that underground plumbing and easily accessible running water are not a reality at this point. We don't know how they fill the jars with water, but we can assume it requires considerable time and effort.

When the jars nearly overflow with *water*, Jesus directs the servants to "draw some out and take it to the master of the feast" (v. 8 ESV). And they do it, knowing what the jars contain—only water.

Did their eyes reveal their confusion? Did they look back and forth between the jars of water and Jesus and the master of the feast?

Surely, serving a glass of water to the man overseeing the celebration when he expects more wine will end badly for everyone involved. Yet, at some point from the jar to the man in charge, what was water turns into wine—wine that causes the master to praise the bridegroom, pleasantly surprised that he had "saved the best till now" (v. 10 NIV).

Jesus's first miracle had, surprisingly, little to do with Him. Somewhere along the way, that water became wine, but Jesus didn't fill the jars. He didn't scoop the water out, nor did He serve it to the master of the feast. The servants did. Regular, ordinary people did what Jesus asked, and something remarkable happened. Servants—they weren't even guests at the party! Jesus invited the servants to play a part in this first miracle.

Maybe these servants were disdained by the people they were serving. Perhaps they lived lives hidden and unnoticed by the masses—unless somebody needed them to do something. Maybe these servants had little hope of any sort of blessed life. This is all conjecture, of course. But we do know that Jesus chose to involve these servants in something they couldn't have done on their own. Let's be clear: Jesus could have done all of it on *His* own. The one who later healed blind, paralyzed, and sick people with a single word or touch and called out a dead man from his tomb—He, without a doubt, could have turned water into wine without anyone else's involvement. And, yet, He chose to involve the most ordinary people at the party.

We don't get to decide through whom and how God works. And, friend, that means you don't get to presume that *you* are too insignificant, too ordinary, too hidden, forgotten, or worthless for God to involve you in His big plan. God doesn't have a list of requirements for you to meet before He asks you to jump into His good work. He's not checking off some list as He considers whether or not you are worthy.

NO SMALL THING

Let's step back further in God's story to understand this better.

All the way back in the Old Testament, when the kingdom of Israel was still in its early years, God allowed His people to have a king. Their king, Saul, looked the part of a king. He was tall, handsome, and quite capable on his own. Yet, when it became clear to God that Saul's heart wasn't for God and God alone, God found a new king.

The new king, God's chosen king, was the youngest, smallest, and most forgettable son of a family full of strapping, hardy, and handsome sons. God's choice even confounded His prophet, Samuel, who was there to find and anoint the new king. When Samuel assumed who the king would be, God corrected him by saying, "Don't judge by his appearance or height, for I have rejected him. The Lord doesn't see things the way you see them. People judge by outward appearance, but the Lord looks at the heart" (1 Samuel 16:7 NLT).

That young, unremarkable son grew up to be the king to whom God would compare every other king. He grew up to make mistakes, yes. Still, he also became a man about whom the apostle Paul, from the New Testament, said God had found a man after His own heart—a man who would do whatever God asked (Acts 13:22). Most notably, God made a covenant with King David, that ordinary, overlooked boy, promising to establish his throne and kingdom forever (2 Samuel 7:16). And we now know that King David's throne will indeed last forever because King Jesus, our everlasting King, hails from the line of David.

Small, ordinary, unremarkable, overlooked, common, regular, hidden—none of that turns God away. None of that disqualifies anyone from the plan and call of God. After all, God is chiefly concerned about and interested in the heart—the part of a person that only He sees and truly knows.

God is looking at your heart, friend. What is He going to find there?

When the Small Things Add Up

Only when we look back can we see more of the story God is writing with our lives. Our vantage point changes. We're no longer in the midst of the everyday trudging, the daily push to make it through, knowing tomorrow would be much the same. From our new vantage point, we can look back and see how all those little things amount to something significant, to something bigger than what felt possible in the beginning.

I can look back at my life and see how so many of the little moments and the small daily decisions have added up to where I am now. All those small choices and changes have brought me here. The nudges and whispers from the Holy Spirit, though slight and easy to explain away, changed my life as I learned to follow and obey.

From my vantage point, a little further along the path of faithfulness than when I started, I can see how the story is beginning to come together. I see common threads and notice how one small thing has led to another. I see it adding up.

Choosing to find the beauty in the everyday and transforming how I viewed even the most mundane, predictable days...

Recognizing my mistake of not prioritizing the Word of God and learning how to fight for my time in it every day (yes, it often was and sometimes still is a fight)...

Realigning my thought life to God's truth and tearing down,

brick by brick, walls and fortresses I had built to protect myself...

Deciding to show up for people even if I didn't feel like it and even if they didn't want it...

Learning to focus on being faithful to God rather than being pleasing or impressive to other people...

The more I said yes (with God's help) to the simple things He asked of me, the more I was ready for whatever was next. The more I stepped out (again, with His help), the more I learned how trustworthy God is. And when it came time for a big yes—a yes that would alter my family's life more than ever before—in some ways, it felt like the most natural thing in the world.

Launch a campus of our church—essentially planting a new church—in a small, easily overlooked town and jump all in, giving of my life, time, and heart?

Yes, God! Yes, I will do that for you.

This was the biggest *yes* of my life—up to that point—and yet, it was also one of the easiest. All the previous and smaller *yeses* paved the way for this big one.

Two and a half years after the initial conversation about launching a new campus, our doors opened for the first time, welcoming the beloved people of a small yet significant town in rural Oklahoma. My husband and I drove back and forth every Sunday and often throughout the week, and we had a committed team of volunteers doing the same. It was a big ask for so many people. It was a hefty leap of faith for our church and the staff involved. It was a defining mountaintop moment for Jamie and me—a moment of extraordinary obedience that had deep roots of the good ol' regular, ordinary kind of obedience. We followed

God's lead one step at a time, and He led us exactly where we needed to be—exactly where He wanted us.

Is It Too Small a Thing?

Are the regular, daily, repetitive steps of obedience too small? That entirely ordinary thing God is asking you to do—is it too small a thing? Is it only the big, audacious things we do for God that matter? Is God only after those climactic moments of impressive obedience?

In a word…no! Oh, I'll say it louder for those in the back… NO!

The Christian life—your life—is not about the big, flashy things you can do for God or even for other people. The life of following Christ is one in which every day matters because your everyday life reveals who you are.

What if the call to lay down your life for Christ, like Jesus asks of Peter in John 13, is less about one heroic moment of giving it all and more about laying your everyday, ordinary life at the feet of Jesus? What if it is choosing to walk through your monotonous and mundane days with such obedience that every little detail is for Him? What if laying down your life looks like a lifetime of small, repetitive, ordinary moments of surrender and obedience?

What if it's *you* in your everyday, sometimes dull, often messy, and always imperfect life that God wants? What if it's *you* that He's after? It's not the things you can do for Him or with Him, but you, your heart, that will please Him the most.

Every small, obedient step matters, friend, because even the most minor moves forward made over a lifetime in the same direction will get you to your King.

Make This Prayer Yours

Lord, I don't always see it as a privilege to obey you. I don't know that I've ever thought of it that way. But I see it now. This is your story—your big, beautiful, incredible story. I'm overwhelmed that you would ask me to participate in it. Would you help me boldly and obediently step out in all the ways you lead me, whether small or not so small? You have done it all and given it all for me. At the very least, my response can be to try to do the same. Help me see even the smallest steps as significant. Help me remember that you are not after one paramount moment of obedience, but rather, you want a lifetime of surrendered steps of obedience. You want my surrendered heart. I give it to you today; help me give it to you tomorrow, the next day, and the day after. In the name of Jesus, amen.

Notes

1. Eugene Peterson's book, *A Long Obedience in the Same Direction*, provides a redefining view of what discipleship and living for God in our fast-paced society could, or even should, look like.

2. Strong's Greek: 1515. εἰρήνη (eiréné) -- one, peace, quietness, rest. Accessed February 25, 2023. https://biblehub.com/greek/1515.htm.

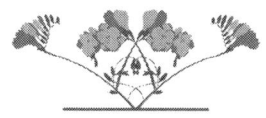

Chapter 10
It's Out of Your Control

There's a picture of my husband, Jamie, that I can't get out of my head. Or I should say a snapshot of his dangling legs because that's all I could see as I walked by our sliding glass door one Saturday afternoon.

It was a beautiful early summer day, perfect for tending to the backyard and doing a little tree trimming. A decent number of shrubs and smaller trees crowded our fence line, and Jamie, annoyed by them, decided it was time to do something about it. As I was folding laundry or cleaning bathrooms or some other indoor chore, he was slowly and methodically trimming back all the shrubs he could get his hands on.

At one point, I walked by, glancing out the sliding glass door to see those dangling legs. He was hanging over the fence, holding onto a tree for dear life. It was the last thing I expected to see. As any kind-hearted wife would do, I laughed. (Although, I wish I had gotten a picture!) Eventually, I stepped outside to check on him, figuring it was what a kind-hearted wife should do.

NO SMALL THING

As he awkwardly righted himself and put his feet back on the ladder underneath him, he told me what he *thought* he was going to do. He *thought* he was going to simply cut down this skinny tree and gather all its limbs in a pile nearby. It looked simple and easy enough. So, he cut the tree at the base—on our side of the fence—and climbed the ladder, hoping to grab the rest, pull it over, and drop it in the pile. He didn't know how big the tree was on the other side of the fence, though. The base of the tree seemed manageable, insignificant even, considering the full-grown trees not far away. The size and weight of this "little" tree, even though he couldn't tell from his vantage point on our side of the fence, was far more than he was expecting. I mean, that tree nearly took him over the fence!

Once he climbed down, having tackled the remainder of the tree to the awaiting pile, we looked up and realized how much of a difference that little tree made. Sunlight streamed in and warmed up what once was an overly shaded portion of our yard. And then we noticed how much shade our neighbors now wouldn't have in their backyard. The impact of removing that little tree was far greater than we had expected. There was no way Jamie could have known just how big that small tree was on the other side of our fence.

Small doesn't mean insignificant.

God had already planted those words in my heart, so it wasn't surprising to me (although it may have been to Jamie) when they came out of my mouth. Just because the tree looked small, it didn't mean it was insignificant. Its size on our side of the fence didn't determine the size of its impact on the other side of the fence.

Just because something feels small, looks small, or even is small doesn't mean the eventual outcome, the result, or impact will be insignificant. This encouraging truth applies to more than just the plant life in our backyard. I'm hoping that is apparent by now, especially since we're nearing the end of our time together.

Actually, it all comes down to this… Our discussion about small things culminates in our conviction that God is the one who determines the significance of those small things. We don't get to decide the result. We don't get to determine the impact. We don't get to arrange the outcome. It's all out of our control. The only thing in our hands to do is what He has asked us to do. Our responsibility is obedience, and everything else is in His infinitely capable hands.

It's out of our control, and, in case you were wondering, that is a good thing!

Our Struggle with Control

At the risk of being too obvious, this chapter directly follows the previous chapter about obedience. (See, I didn't tell you anything new there.) What may not be quite as obvious is that a discussion about control is an apt follow-up to that of one about obedience. A fully surrendered and obedient heart requires a release of control. Isn't that what surrender implies?

While this won't be a deep dive into the subject of control—our obsession with it and God's sole possession of it—it is necessary to wade into it for a few minutes. Sharon Hodde Miller recently wrote an entire book discussing the very high cost of control, and she wisely tells us that "control is a God category, not a human one." Yet, because of technology, we have lost our awareness of just how out of control we are. We live with an "illusion of control," she says. And to further the point, she adds, "Our spiritual muscles of trust, of surrender, and of accepting our limitations have atrophied. Likewise, our senses of smallness and frailty feel terrifyingly foreign whenever we encounter them."[1]

Control belongs to God. He alone is sovereign. He alone knows it all. He alone created everything we see and everything we cannot see. (Yes, I'll keep bringing up Genesis 1:1!) He is the author of His big story. We are not. When we attempt to write our own plot lines and outcomes, we, ultimately, are grasping for something we could never attain or maintain—control.

Our struggle for control doesn't always look like a rebellious vying for what isn't ours, though. It can slip by under the guise of insecurity and doubt—not an all-out mutiny, but rather a slow, gentle slide toward idleness, apathy, and eventual refusal to obey.

We may be familiar with this kind of control, but I doubt we have labeled it as such. Instead, we classify it as "I want to be sure" or "I'm still praying about it" or "I don't want to make a mistake or get it wrong." These aren't incorrect in and of themselves, but when surrender and obedience are withheld until we have absolute certainty, we're verging on God's territory. Only He can know with absolute certainty. What He asks of us is to trust Him—even amid uncertainty.

I don't know where the line is—the line between faithfully waiting and fearfully procrastinating. Maybe it moves with every circumstance or shifts as we mature in our walk with Christ. But I know it's there, and I've crossed it too many times to count. I've held back from taking a step because I was afraid of the outcome, of what other people would think, or of failing. I've even prolonged obedience because I was afraid of succeeding. In each circumstance, I wanted to know what would happen on the other side of my obedience. I wanted to see what was on the other side of the fence before I cut the tree.

IT'S OUT OF YOUR CONTROL

Our Christian life, the journey along the path of faithfulness, is one in which we relinquish our need for control, for knowing what's going to happen, and replace it with our confidence in the One who directs our every step, delights in the details along the way, and holds our hand through it all (Psalm 37:23-24). And just like any other journey, it's one step at a time—one foot in front of the other.

When It Doesn't Make Sense

In the book of Acts, we read about the exploits of the apostles and followers of Jesus Christ during the onset of the early church. There's one particular account involving a man named Philip, God's leading, and an unexpected place that showcases what it looks like to follow God even when it doesn't make sense. In Acts 8, we learn this about Philip:

> Philip went down to the city of Samaria and proclaimed to them the Christ. And the crowds with one accord paid attention to what was being said by Philip, when they heard him and saw the signs that he did. For unclean spirits, crying out with a loud voice, came out of many who had them, and many who were paralyzed or lame were healed. So there was much joy in that city (vs. 5-8 ESV).

Philip, one of the very first missionaries, is preaching and proclaiming the good news of Jesus Christ in Samaria—drawing crowds and experiencing mighty miracles. Lives are being changed. People are being healed and set free. The entire city is being affected. This is significant work with successful results! Great momentum is building as the gospel spreads throughout the region.

However, in the middle of this great success, God asks Philip to leave it and go somewhere unexpected. God says, "Rise and go toward the south to the road that goes down from Jerusalem to Gaza" (v. 26 ESV). The text reveals Philip's destination as a "desert place." A desolate place. A lonely place. A less-traveled place. A place of seeming insignificance, especially compared to what was happening in Samaria.

Yet, Philip obediently rises and goes. Philip travels to the desert place.

Does it make sense? Probably not. Does it seem like the next right thing to do? My guess is no. Does Philip know what is ahead for him? I don't think so. Does that hold him back? No.

Wait until you hear what happens next!

Philip encounters a man, "an Ethiopian, a eunuch, a court official of Candace, queen of the Ethiopians, who was in charge of all her treasure" (v. 27 ESV). This man is reading from the scroll of Isaiah, and as Philip hears him, the Holy Spirit urges Philip to join him. Right there, in the Ethiopian man's chariot and in this desert place, Philip reveals the very good news of Jesus Christ, changing the man's life forever. When they approach some water, the Ethiopian man asks to be baptized. So, they climb out of the chariot and into the water. As soon as the newly baptized man emerges from the water, Philip is carried away by the Spirit. They never see each other again.

That's it. Philip travels to this desert place for that one man. God sends Philip from a place of considerable success toward a forgotten, overlooked, insignificant place for that one Ethiopian man. One. Single. Solitary. Small. But not insignificant.

Even if the Ethiopian man were just a regular Joe walking along this dusty road, he would have been significant enough

IT'S OUT OF YOUR CONTROL

for God to orchestrate Philip's arrival. Many of Jesus's parables revealed His love for and determination to pursue the one: The shepherd who leaves the ninety-nine sheep to find the missing one. The joy of the woman who finds her one lost coin. The man who celebrates the return of his wayward son. Not only that, but Jesus repeatedly sought after, comforted, and took time for the one during His ministry on Earth: The one woman at the well. The one tax collector, Zacchaeus, in the tree. He *touched* a leprous man. He stopped to heal one woman with an issue of blood in an overwhelming crowd. He stepped in and offered mercy and forgiveness to an adulterous woman as stones were aimed at her head. One *is* significant.

But this man was not just anybody on that desert road. He was a court official of the Queen of Ethiopia. In some capacity, he had influence. We don't know what happened to this man after his encounter with Philip. But is it too much to assume this one man could have had a significant impact on the gospel of Jesus Christ making its way to Africa? Who knows what this one moment in a desert place may have sparked for an entire country of people!

Philip's act of obedience, following God even when it didn't quite make sense, may have rippled into something bigger than he could ever have imagined or planned on his own. Actually, I'm going to say it probably did.

If this were a Bible study, we'd camp out here longer because there's more to glean from this brief encounter. For our purpose today, though, we can walk away encouraged by Philip's obedience and willingness to venture out into the unknown. We can recognize the significant impact obedience can have, whether or not we get to experience it or even know about it.

What's your desert place? Where has God been calling you?

What has God been asking you to do? What step do you need to take today?

Maybe it's reaching out to someone you haven't talked to in years, and the last time you did speak, it didn't go well. Maybe you know she is holding a grudge against you…or perhaps you are the one holding the grudge. She hasn't reached out. She doesn't seem to care, so why should you? You both have gone your ways and could easily leave well enough alone. Sure, that makes sense, except you can't stop thinking about her.

You may be feeling a tug toward a different job. You are secure where you are, but you can't shake the feeling that it's time to go. It would mean leaving your coworkers, benefits, and comfort, too. And who knows if the other job would even compare? But there's a constant nudge in your heart that it's time to step out now.

Maybe you feel compelled to give someone twenty dollars. You may have the urge to pay for the groceries of the lady behind you in line. Maybe God is asking you to start volunteering in your local school district.

Whatever it is, if God is behind it, it will be worth it. You may not see the results or understand the why, but ultimately, that's not your job. May you be like Philip; may you boldly rise up and go.

Finding Freedom on the Other Side

The thing about walking in this life-altering-kind-of surrender and obedience, fully trusting God to be who He is and do what He does, is that there are few physical guarantees. Assurances about our God, however, are aplenty. We can be sure He will be with us (Psalm 23; Matthew 28:20). We can be sure He will lead us along the way (Proverbs 3:5-6). We can be sure He will help us

IT'S OUT OF YOUR CONTROL

(The Holy Spirit, John 14:15-16). We can be sure God is always faithful (Psalm 119:90; 2 Timothy 2:13). The list could go on!

Specific guarantees concerning our lives are offered less generously in the Word of God. When God invites us to follow Him, He asks us to trust that every guarantee we need will be found in Him. Can that be enough for us? In the day and age of helicopter parenting, googling every medical symptom, compulsive refreshing of our social media feeds, and obsession with political prophecies[2], can we surrender and obey wherever God leads, trusting He knows what is ahead even though we don't?

Can we let go of control?

Now, hear me out… Of course, there will be times when we are tempted to grapple for control, even now that we have put a name to it. Psalm 131, a short, poignant Psalm of David, offers us a prayer and hope for those times. The first two verses read:

> O Lord, my heart is not lifted up;
> > my eyes are not raised too high;
> I do not occupy myself with things
> > too great and too marvelous for me.
> But I have calmed and quieted my soul,
> > like a weaned child with its mother;
> > like a weaned child is my soul within me.

"I have calmed and quieted my soul," David says. I'm not reaching and grasping for what is out of my control. I know my place. I'm secure in my position as the one who surrenders and obeys. I am at peace—the kind of peace a child experiences with her mother, not needing or wanting anything from her. The stability of a child convinced of how thoroughly loved she is.

Letting go of control leads to a calm, quieted soul—a heart

at peace. A heart at peace knows its place and does only what it is tasked to do. A calmed and quieted soul is convinced of God's overwhelming goodness and ability to accurately determine the significance and outcome of every little thing surrendered to Him.

At the core of a calmed and quieted soul, we find something for which we are all desperately seeking. We find freedom. Freedom from striving. Freedom from fear. Freedom from proving ourselves. Freedom from insecurity. Freedom from what other people think and say about us. Freedom from pleasing people. Freedom from performing. We find the freedom to be and do precisely what God created us to be and do.

Knowing that freedom is there doesn't automatically make it ours, however. It doesn't mean we won't struggle with striving and insecurity. It doesn't mean all the fear disappears, never to return. It means we know it's not our fight. It means we know who's on our side—or, more accurately, whose side we are on. It means we know we can stand on all those guarantees of who our God is and what He does for us. It means we know the fear, insecurity, and anxiety aren't ours to claim. It means we know our God is bigger, and we find our freedom in Him!

When our minds and hearts aren't wrapped up in determining our steps and the outcome of those steps, we are free to surrender, obey, and follow wherever He leads. Letting go of control, letting go of our need for certainty, speaks to our faith in our big God. It reveals our trust in His big plan and the big, unshakable hope He offers us. Letting go of control is like that trust fall we talked about in the previous chapter. We can let go; we can jump because we know who is there to catch us.

Ultimately, relinquishing control keeps us on the path of faithfulness. It's God's path, after all. It's the ancient way He set out for us long ago. It's the course Adam and Eve failed to follow. It's the path humanity (as a whole) has bucked against, run away from, and refused to follow ever since that infamous day in the garden. Finding and following that path requires surrendering our own path and way of living, and it wouldn't be possible without letting go of control.

In Psalm 119, we discover that walking along God's path requires obedience to what God has laid out as right and true in His Law, His Word. And we also find the connection to freedom:

> I will keep on obeying your instructions
> > forever and ever.
> I will walk in freedom,
> > for I have devoted myself to your commandments
> (vs. 44-45 NLT).

Freedom is found on the other side of letting go, on the other side of surrender. Freedom is found on the other side of devotion and obedience to His way. Freedom is found as we learn to trust Him and His big, beautiful plan.

When we are bent on knowing what is on the other side of whatever God asks us to do, may we remember that freedom is there. If God asks it, He will see to it until the end. And that's the best freedom of all!

When We Don't See the Fruit

We have a little grove of fruit trees in our current backyard—not the one with the sliding glass door and missing tree. I like to call it a grove because it sounds so picturesque. But, in reality, it's a strip of our backyard where previous homeowners planted two rows of a few different fruit trees. It's *maybe* eight trees in total. Let's call it a mini grove.

NO SMALL THING

Every year, when the trees begin to yawn, stretch, and wake up from their winter slumber, the sprigs of new life, the unfurling baby leaves, and the burgeoning blossoms teach me something new. As the flowers bloom and fruit—actual fruit—bursts forth, all the imagery found within Scripture of flourishing trees and abundant life floods through my mind. Every year. It's a jaw-dropping reminder of how wonderful and intricate our God is!

The first summer we lived in our home, we had no idea what to expect from our fruit trees. We bought our house from people we knew, but they had only lived here for a few months, during the fall and winter. They didn't know much about the trees; they couldn't even tell us what they were. They never saw the fruit.

One hot summer day, I grabbed a little black wire basket from the pantry and slipped out the back door. I was going to harvest some fruit from my fruit trees! I filled that basket to the brim with warm, slightly squishy, golden plums. (That's what an app told me they were.) What a bounty! I even took a picture…of course, I did!

In that moment, God made something obvious to me: We don't always get to reap the harvest of seeds we plant.

Sometimes we don't see the fruit of prayers we pray for people, the words of encouragement we speak to someone, the smile, the kind gesture, the little things we do. Sometimes we don't experience the fruit of our obedience, the big or small steps we take, or the decisions we make. Sometimes we don't know the outcome of what God asked us to put into motion.

But that doesn't mean there isn't fruit. That doesn't mean there isn't significance.

I didn't plant the seeds for the plums overflowing my little wire basket. I didn't plant any of the fruit-filled trees in my backyard.

IT'S OUT OF YOUR CONTROL

Someone else planted them a few years earlier, but they moved before they could enjoy the fruits of their labor. (It takes years before fruit trees bear fruit, and our trees aren't very old yet.) Even our friends, who lived here before us, never experienced the harvest of those trees.

My family munched on those plums all summer. I even attempted to make plum jam. (It didn't turn out too well.) Someone else sowed the seeds and planted the trees, but we reaped the harvest. They planted, believing the trees would produce, even though they couldn't see it yet—even though they never got to see it.[3]

I don't know about you, but I want to live like that! It's the planting and the tiny seeds that matter. It's the starting. Doing the thing. And then trusting that the harvest will be what and when it is supposed to be—by the grace and power of God.

It reminds me of what the apostle Paul tells the Corinthian church in 1 Corinthians 3: "I planted, Apollos watered, but God gave the growth" (v. 6 ESV). Sometimes we may be the ones who plant. Other times, we may be the ones who water. Maybe we'll even be the ones who get to experience the fruit! But it is God who does the growing. God determines the outcome and the significance of it.

So, friend, let's be encouraged by my little grove of fruit trees. Let's determine to plant or water to the best of our ability and trust that God knows exactly what He is doing. Let's trust God to bring about the fruit whenever and however He deems appropriate. He is the Master Gardener, after all.

Into the Unknown We Go

Saying yes to the call to lead a new church in a little town (even though it went against everything we had been taught) was the easy part. Agreeing to the time and commitment it would require—emotionally, spiritually, and physically—was almost second nature. However, the decision to uproot our kids and plant our whole lives into a community with limited resources and opportunities proved more daunting. Truthfully, it required a new level of surrender.

The driving back-and-forth rhythm we had adopted was inconvenient but entirely doable. The drive was easy and beautiful—open land and open skies, fields dotted with grazing cattle, and rolling hills covered in trees that changed with the seasons. And at certain times of the year, we were accompanied by stunning sunsets on our drive home. Truly, it was not a hardship.

However, as time progressed and our church family grew, the draw to plant our roots where our hearts already resided became too strong to ignore. God was calling us to our new home—a tiny town with one blinking stoplight and only a handful of restaurants. Our biggest concern and point of contention were our kids, two of whom were in the unpredictable and vulnerable middle school years.

Control tried to sneak in, and it was in the shape of a legitimate concern for our children. We struggled with it. We were worried about the possibility of our kids being negatively affected by our obedience to the Lord. We wanted certainty. We wanted a guarantee that our kids would thrive.

Eventually, it was a single question Jamie sensed God asking that put us at ease. It reminded us to calm and quiet our souls.

IT'S OUT OF YOUR CONTROL

God asked him, "Can you trust me with your children?" That was it. Did we trust Him? Sure, over the years, we had learned to trust Him with our finances, jobs, and ministry opportunities. We knew Him to be the provider in those areas. So, why would we question Him when it came to the well-being of our kids?

Can you trust me with your children?

Can you trust me with that which is most precious to you?

Can you trust that what is precious to you is even more precious to me?

With hands up and hearts surrendered, Jamie and I said yes. It was the biggest yes we've ever said, leading us somewhere smaller than we would have planned for ourselves. Yet, this modest town and the people who call it home have changed our lives more than we could have dreamed. Our hearts are full. Our lives are brimming with love, excitement, and utter gratitude about what God is doing in our small town.

Lest you think it's all butterflies and roses, however, we're still leaning on God—trusting that He's holding onto our kids and won't let go. And when it comes to our church, we're still holding onto God's irrefutable call to do what we are doing, to be where we are. We're still walking in the unknown.

What is the outcome of our decision going to be years from now—for our family, for our little town, for our church family? We don't know.

What kind of impact will the steps we have taken and will continue to take have on those around us? We don't know. And, honestly, it isn't for us to know.

When our eyes, time, and attention are more focused on what may be ahead, we're less focused on and grateful for what is here and now. Here and now is what we have and where we are. We never want to lose sight of that.

We don't know what's on the other side of the fence. We don't know how the years ahead will unfold, but we know who does. And we've decided that's enough for us. We know He's a big God (who is ever so close) with a big plan (for our eventual good—whatever that may be), and we are saturated with unshakable, confident hope for what is ahead.

Is It Too Small a Thing?

However God sees fit to work the outcome of your obedience—is that too small a thing? Or, just knowing that He is at work—is that not enough? How about the significance of even the littlest things you do—does it not matter?

Whatever God determines the impact and significance of your steps of obedience to be—is it too small a thing? Is the freedom you can find on the other side of surrendering too small a thing?

No! (You knew that answer!)

It is no small thing. Whatever the outcome and whatever the significance, it matters. Whether it affects one or one hundred thousand, it matters. Whether it lasts for one day or one hundred years, it matters. Whether big or small, the significance of your steps and your obedience matters.

The years you dedicate to raising your children—feeling hidden away, constantly washing, cooking, or cleaning—matter.

The commitment to taking your growing children to church

IT'S OUT OF YOUR CONTROL

every Sunday—whether you see any positive results or not—matters.

Saying "no" to your fear, joining a small group, and sticking with it— even if you don't know (yet) anyone who attends—matters.

We've gone through lists like this many times in this book:

Showing up.

Reaching out.

Simply saying hi to someone.

Picking up your Bible as often as you can.

Praying (even if for just a few minutes).

Saying yes when you can.

Making a meal for someone.

Learning your neighbors' names.

Working hard at what may feel like a dead-end job.

Doing your best for someone who barely notices you at all.

Watching your words.

Guarding your thoughts.

It all matters. It is all significant, some even more than we may ever know.

Who are we to put a limit on how a friendly smile can change someone's day? Who are we to limit the power of a simple prayer? To define what one little, ordinary thing can lead to, can do in our own lives or the lives of people around us?

I don't know about you, but I do not want to be caught trying to limit what our big, almighty, infinite God wants to do in and through me. I don't want to grapple for the control that isn't mine to hold onto in the first place. God is God, and I am not. Thank goodness for that!

Our job is simple: We obey. We do the thing—big or small. The outcome, the significance, and the impact belong to God. He will see to the success of that which He has called us to do, and He determines the significance of that success. In the end, our success is found in our surrendering. Our success is our obedience.

Make This Prayer Yours

Lord, my first step is to admit I struggle with control. It's hard not to know what is on the other side of what you ask me to do. I realize that when I waver and hold back out of insecurity or fear, I'm actually trying to do your job. I'm grasping for control. I'm sorry! Lord, help me move forward, trusting you. Help me take the steps you would have me take. Help me let go of control, and help me be okay with the unknown. I may not always know what is ahead, but I know Who is ahead…You! Today, I surrender to your will. I will obey your way, and I will go where you lead. I trust you! And I trust you to do what you will with what I do for you. The significance and outcome are out of my control. I will simply obey. Lord, help me obey. In the name of Jesus, amen.

IT'S OUT OF YOUR CONTROL

Notes

1. Sharon Hodde Miller, *The Cost of Control: Why We Crave It, the Anxiety It Gives Us, and the Real Power God Promises* (Grand Rapids, Michigan: Baker Books, 2022), chap. 2, Scribd.

2. Note about prophecy: I believe in and desire it, but at some point, an obsession with prophecy becomes a trap for control. It's an illusion of control.

3. I originally wrote about this and posted a picture of the plums on Instagram in 2021. It can be found at instagram.com/ashleylainekelly.

Bathsheba's Story

Found in 2 Samuel 11 and 12

How could this have happened?

What did I do to cause this?

Wait…do I even matter?

It was evening. Bathsheba was on the roof, bathing and purifying herself as was required at the end of every menstrual cycle. How many times had she done this before? Countless. It was completely ordinary and routine.

This time was different, however. All of a sudden, men appeared, interrupting her bathing. Whether they came in cautiously or with force, we do not know. Either way, Bathsheba was exposed and subjected to whatever they required because they were the king's men. They had been sent for her. King David had summoned her.

The king. How could she not go? Did she have a choice? There's only one reason a man, especially of his status, would call for a woman—a married woman, mind you—at this time in the evening. And the king gets what he wants.

Weeks later, when Bathsheba discovered she would not need a purification bath for nine months, she sent word to King David. One moment, out of her control, and life was forever changed. And now she waited.

BATHSHEBA'S STORY

How could this have happened?

What did I do to cause this?

Wait…do I even matter?

Bathsheba was the wife of Uriah, one of King David's soldiers away at battle. The tiny baby growing inside her could have only belonged to the king; he knew that. What could be done?

King David tried to bring together Uriah and Bathsheba, attempting to cover his tracks. But Uriah was committed and dedicated to King David and the men fighting far from their wives. He would not enjoy a privilege the other men did not have. Eventually, in desperation, David made a repugnant decision—to have Uriah killed in battle. He *tried* to cover his sin with the death of an innocent man.

In all of this, we don't know Bathsheba's state of mind. Did she love Uriah? Did she sincerely grieve his death? Every decision was taken from her. Every step was made for her. The way forward now was to marry King David and give birth to his child, a son.

If only that were where it stopped…or where it turned around for Bathsheba. The child whom Bathsheba bore and loved died. He died. The pain. The agony. The grief of the loss of what life was supposed to be, of what it could have been. How had it come to this?

Thankfully, her story doesn't stop there…

Conclusion
It Is No Small Thing

I don't know if you caught it, but I showed you all my cards right from the start. Before you even cracked the spine of this book or read the first page, I revealed the big "aha" moment. The title says it all.

No Small Thing.

If that wasn't enough, the introduction pointed you to this essential truth: Small doesn't mean insignificant. Plus, each chapter along the way boldly claimed: It is no small thing.

It has been my goal to help you clear your vision. To help you shift and realign your perspective. To help you more clearly see your life through the lens God has put in place. That lens, of course, is your big God, His big plan, and the big hope you have in Him.

I pray—seriously and very sincerely—that God has used this book, these pages filled with words straight from my heart, to do two things. One, to fill you with greater awe and wonder of your vast and mighty God—who He is and all He has done and

IT IS NO SMALL THING

continues to do. And two, to encourage, embolden, and inspire you to awaken to the life He is calling you to live—right where you are, when you are, and with what you have.

When it comes to living the life God has created you to live, there is nothing too small, trivial, insignificant, hidden, ordinary, or worthless. Not only that, but you are not too small, trivial, insignificant, hidden, ordinary, or worthless. Your big God isn't in the business of making insignificant things. It all has purpose; *you* have purpose.

Your purpose is to know, love, and live for Him. It is the path of life, the path of faithfulness.

Remember that the sum of your life, the path you take, is what you do every day. Right here, right now is the stuff of life. The life you have *now* is what you have been given and when you have been placed to live for God—to live for His glory and the good of His people. Right here. Right now. No matter how small you feel. No matter how inadequate you think you are. No matter what you have or don't have. No matter who is in your life or not. No matter what.

While you endeavor to live a life that continually asks whether it is *too small a thing*, I hope you now understand what the answer should always be: It is no small thing.

It is no small thing who God is, what He has done, and the hope He offers. It is no small thing what is in front of you, and it is no small thing what God is asking of you. From this point forward, may you be a "no small thing" person!

Is it too small a thing? No. No, it is not.

Tamar, Rahab, Ruth, and Bathsheba

Before we say goodbye, I have one final story to tell, or finish telling, you. What began as four stories of four ordinary women will now end as one story. It's a long-game kind of story. A story God weaved throughout *His* story. The culmination is found in an unexpected, often overlooked place—the genealogy at the beginning of the Gospel of Matthew.

Matthew begins his Gospel with the genealogy of Jesus Christ. This is where we read, "Abraham was the father of Isaac," and so-and-so was the father of this other so-and-so and on and on (1:2). It continues repetitively, and naturally, our eyes tend to glaze over as we try to pronounce the peculiar names. But, as is appropriate to the entire message of this book, there is plenty of beauty and significance to be found in the monotony of the names.

Four names stand out and are different in a very particular way: "...and Judah the father of Perez and Zerah by *Tamar*...and Salmon the father of Boaz by *Rahab*, and Boaz the father of Obed by *Ruth*...and David was the father of Solomon by *the wife of Uriah*..." (vs. 3, 5-6 ESV, emphasis added). Tamar. Rahab. Ruth. Bathsheba—the wife of Uriah. Only four women are included in the genealogy of Christ—other than Mary, of course. That is significant.

Tamar was forgotten and treated as worthless. And, yet, here she shows up in a place of significant worth. Rahab was one woman who made a difference...a big enough difference to find a place among the ancestors of Jesus Christ. Ruth had little hope and few prospects but remained loyal and obedient even when it didn't make sense. She had no way of knowing her part in the story that would eventually give hope to all. And Bathsheba—her life not her own, yet she holds a place of honor in the bigger story that has lasted thousands of years.

Their stories were full of brokenness, questions, pain, and many unknowns, but that is not where they ended.

Long after they had lived and loved, long after they had breathed their last breath, and long after every little thing they did, their stories continued to weave in and out of God's big, beautiful story. Their names and their significance lived on in their descendants, and eventually, the One who had been promised all the way back in Genesis 3 was born. Their stories became part of the most incredible story ever told, ever lived.

There's no way these four ordinary women knew what God would do with what little they had to offer. There's no way they knew how God would shape their stories. There's no way these four ordinary women knew what the outcome of their simple, regular, day-to-day lives would be. There's no way they knew the part they were playing in God's big, beautiful, life-changing, life-redeeming plan.

God knew what He was doing. It was a long game, but, goodness, look at how good at it He is!

No Small Thing Manifesto

My God is a big, mighty, immeasurable God who is ever so close to me. My big God has a big plan. In fact, He's playing the long game, and He's exceptionally good at it. My big God's big plan ends with the biggest hope of all: He'll be forever again with us, with me. Because of my big God, His big plan, and this big hope, I can live my life now assured that *I* matter and what I *do* matters. I find freedom in trusting and obeying my vast and mighty God. I find significance in my every day because it's a day He has given

NO SMALL THING

me. Every single, ordinary, regular day, I have the privilege to know Him, love Him, and live for Him. That is no small thing!

NOW, I BOLDLY PROCLAIM: IT IS NO SMALL THING!

- It is no small thing who my God is and what He has done for me.
- It is no small thing who God has made me to be and the life He has given me.
- It is no small thing—my everyday, ordinary, routine life.
- It is no small thing—the daily, repetitive, small steps I take toward Him.
- It is no small thing what I can do for others right where I am now and with what I have.
- It is no small thing how God chooses to speak to and guide me.
- It is no small thing when I obey Him and surrender to His way.
- It is no small thing whatever the outcome and results may be.
- My life here and now—every day, every step, every choice—is my gift to God. It is no small thing.

Dear Reader

It is important to me that you know the book you hold in your hands and all the words you have read from me are my attempt at putting everything I have encouraged you to do into action. This is my "no small thing" act of obedience and surrender.

I am unknown in the literary world and the Christian author and Bible teacher world. I do not have a large platform. Nor do I have a sizable following or email list. There will not be thousands of people lining up to buy this book or influencing others about it on social media. In the eyes of the world (even the Christian world), I am small. This book is small.

But it is not insignificant.

If you are the only one to read these words, it will have been worth it. If you are the only one to act on what was written here, it will have been worth it. If you are the only one to take on this call to be a "no small thing" person, it will have been worth it. Because you, my friend, are worth it. You are not insignificant.

There is no small thing regarding the Kingdom of God and what He asks us to do. I'm forever grateful God opened my eyes and heart to see this remarkable truth in His Word and life. More than that, though, I'm thankful He is helping me live it out.

There is no small thing, friend. That includes you and your life, too.

For His glory and the good of His people,

Ashley

Acknowledgments

I don't even know how to begin with these acknowledgments. First, let me put this out there: I will inevitably forget someone or leave people out that should be included here. So, please forgive me. I will do my best.

Mom and Dad: This whole book is steeped in your faithfulness, your integrity, and your unconditional love. You have flavored my story and my words more than anyone else (except God Himself, of course). Through all my ups and downs in those early years of adulthood, I never once questioned your love or support for me. I only ever knew home as a safe place—a place I could always return to no matter what. I'm convinced my faith in God is only stronger because of how you modeled His love to me. Thank you. I don't say it enough, but I'm declaring it for anyone and everyone to read now. Thank you. I love you.

Jamie: How can my words adequately express what I want to say? You are the best man I know. Period. Your heart for people, for God, and for your family is bigger than most people know, even though they often see a large part of it on your sleeve. Thank you for who you are. (Thank you, God, for making Jamie the way You did.) Who would have thought a boy from Minnesota would meet a girl from Oklahoma and fall head over heels in love? A Minnesota boy was never in my dreams until I met you, and then, somehow, it just felt like you were my dream all along. I love our life. The simple, everyday, routine of it all—the highs, the lows, and, especially, the somewhere-in-betweens. One thing is for certain: Neither of us know what God has in store. If it is anything like the past sixteen years, though, we're in for quite a ride! And there's no one I'd rather be buckled up next to. I love you.

Averley, Paycen, and Camden: My ever-growing children—I love you. It's been the supreme joy of my life to watch you grow (and to grow right alongside you)! God has taught me about life and His ways and His love through each of you. When you read this book and all that God has done in my life, my hope is that you will see Him more and see Him bigger in your story, too. Every word is for you. And, hey, guess what… You can follow your dreams. You can do big things, and you can do small things. All of it matters—just remember to keep your heart squarely in the hands of your Heavenly Father. (Good news: He'll hold onto you, too! You don't have to do it on your own.)

Whitley: What can I say? You're my number one cheerleader. You're my ride or die—although we've never called each other that. We've come a long way since those early years when I wouldn't let you talk. Now, you're the one who usually has to push me to talk. Funny how that works! Thank you for putting up with me all these years. Thank you for not giving up on me, too. I love you!

My family (still on earth): For those of you who have known about this project, thank you for your support and excitement. I'm not sure I deserve it, but I sure do appreciate it. For those of you who may never read this book, I'm still thankful for your love and place in my life. You belong here, too.

My family (no longer on earth): I didn't intend to talk about you so much. I had no idea how your losses had shaped me over the years, but I'm thankful I know now. I'm holding onto the hope of seeing you again (and seeing some of you for the first time).

What a joyous day that will be!

Pastors Scott and Mary: Thank you for the years you have poured into our church and into my life. Your support and trust have propelled me further in ministry and my own path of faithfulness. Thank you for allowing me to grow, for creating space for me, and for encouraging me forward.

Our Pawhuska peeps: Each and everyone of you has changed my life for the better. Jamie and I would have never guessed Pawhuska, Oklahoma, was in the cards for us, but we are beyond grateful it is. We are grateful YOU are. We're two and a half years into this adventure, but, at the same time, it feels like we've been here our whole lives. Thank you for welcoming us. Thank you for loving us. Thank you for coming back to church again and again. Most weeks, we're convinced it is only God who is bringing you all back! What is God up to in Pawhuska, Oklahoma, and all of Osage County? I know we all feel it! Here in Pawhuska as it is in Heaven.

Friends, near and far: If you have thought of me, if you have encouraged me, if you have prayed for me, and if you have talked with me about this book, you are included here. There are too many of you to name, but I'm unbelievably grateful and humbled by your support and encouragement and prayers. To those who continually asked me how the writing process was going, thank you. You made this feel real. To those who have dreamed about this book with me, thank you. To those who celebrated with me when the writing was finished, thank you. To those who have requested to celebrate with me once the book is released, thank you. I'm not much of a party thrower, but I guess it's time to throw a party! To those who have prayed for years about this book, thank you. It is no small thing. I truly, wholeheartedly believe that.

About the Author

ASHLEY KELLY is a pastor's wife, writer, Bible teacher, and speaker. Years of leading in the church—small groups, Bible studies, and children's and women's ministries—have ignited her passion to help believers more fully know and love God as they begin to more fully know, love, and live out the Word of God.

Ashley and her husband, Jamie, live in and lead a church campus in Pawhuska, Oklahoma—a small town filled with the best people. They have three children who refuse to stop growing but graciously still cozy up on the couch for family movie nights.

Connect with her and find more information on her website and Instagram: RootedandStrong.com and @ashleylainekelly

Made in the USA
Monee, IL
11 August 2023